HEALING TH

MW00896919

Habits that will shift you from a "Morgue" mentality to a "Forbes" mentality.

By Keyon Clinton

ISBN-13:978-1722923754

ISBN-10:172292375X

TABLE OF CONTENTS

DEDICATION

First, I would like to give an honor to God who is the head of my life!

To my mother, my superman, you are truly my greatest inspiration in life. Raising 4 boys to the best of your ability and sacrificing your dreams so that we can live out ours is what makes you a super mom. I could not ask God for a better mom. You will always be my first queen and my promise of retiring you and buying you a home when I was 14 still stands. I love you for everything that you have done for my brothers and I. Love you Ma.

I would like to also dedicate this book Coach Coker. You were the lifeline to what most people would call a dead community. Without your love, investments and genuine care to see me succeed I am not sure where my life would have ended up. Although the Lord called you home to his kingdom of heaven I will never forget the plethora of lessons you have taught to me on how to persevere through adversity. I'll never forget these sweet words from your voice: "Character is doing the right thing because it is the right thing to do"! Thank you for believing in a little boy from an impoverished community.

ACKNOWLEDGEMENTS

Thank you to each individual below because without you and your influence on my life this book could not have been written:

Michelle Clinton, Leon Tyner, Antonio Clinton, Leon Clinton, Deon Clinton, George Coker, Deon'ta Bailey, Darius Barrett, Trammel Brown, D'Andre Jackson, Roxanne Fantroy, Cherfona Fantroy, Antoine Fantroy, Anthony Fantroy, Tara Clinton, Claire Clinton, Mattie Clinton, Kimberly Garrison, Tuk Garrison, Savoy Garrison, Albert Garrison, Micheal Garrison, Kaneesha Garrison, Antoine Garrison, Donald Mingus, Donna Mingus, Donald Mingus, Dinah Mingus, Shawn Fair, Shawn T. Blanchard, Jose Anderson, Bianca Benguche, Amber Clinton, Deon Clinton Jr, Karie Clinton, Kaleb Clinton, Keith Barnes, Paris Wilson, Justin Dunn, Kevin Jackson, Denzell Wright, Henry Ward, Kenneth Jackson, Brannon Bass, Veotis Thompson, Tyler Hendon, Tyler Clifford Dedrick Cotton II, Marvin Harbour, Charles Colson, Bryan Cotton, Theodore Caldwell.

FOREWARD

Keyon Clinton is a good friend of mine that is unbelievably skilled, talented and gifted. I have personally witnessed him demonstrate the ability to bring the absolute best out of people that have crossed his path. He is a man who has power to lead and maintain a humble spirit that draws people to a light the pierces the heart.

The profundity of Keyon's information and the adequacy of his conveyance style put him in a unique position to influence his peers and those who came before him. His love for people is unquestionable and his desire to see everyone lead a spirit filled life is a mission that he has already begun to execute.

In this book, Keyon observes that people are physically alive but mentally and morally dead hence they are walking around with no true purpose in life. He wrote the book "Healing The Living Dead" to help readers build up self-confidence and give them the strength and confidence to face life struggles. Keyon aim is to give his audience the spirit of "never say never" hence you must not give up.

Be well assured that you will be inspired after reading this book. There are excessive numbers of individuals who are physically alive yet rationally and ethically dead. Strolling around with no reason or plan throughout everyday life. This book will feature Keyon's excursion and declaration to rouse everybody that regardless of how dull your past is, you can influence your future as brilliant as you to need it to be.

The state of the healing the living dead is a tip on how to be successful in life and peace that established when readers allow God to lead their lives. This is why putting God first in everything that you do will increase your level of perspective. Having a spiritual connection with a higher source allows your mind, body, and soul to flourish in ways that the human mind cannot fathom. The vision you get from God never diminishes. Just like there are specific parameters we need to elevate in the air, we must have parameters to advance in God. Spiritually when we try to promote in God, the enemy tries to hold us down. I am a firm believer that if God is the primary source of any endeavor in your life, it will work out in your favor.

Keyon provide every reader with love, inspiration, motivation, direction and the key to living a life with purpose by helping tap into the ultimate source of our being which is Our Father, Jesus Christ.

Forbes Coaching Council Member, International
Motivational Speaker, Fair Consulting Group; CEO

PHASE 1: RESURRECTION

CHAPTER 1: THE INFAMOUS ZIP CODE

48205 Is Detroit's High Crime Neighborhood… It's Also Home To The Largest Share Of Poor People And It's Now Targeted For The Brunt Of Welfare Benefit Cuts.

The *Detroit News* reported on September 30, 2011, that the most dangerous neighborhood in America is most likely Detroit MI, 48205. At least 38 people were shot and 8 died from the first day of summer, June 21, 2011, to August, 21, 2011, in the 48205 ZIP code. A 6.5-square-mile slice of the city north of Coleman A. Young International Airport roughly bordered by Eight Mile, Hoover, Conner and Kelly. Gangs have caused big problems at Osborn High School on Seven Mile and Hoover, according to an April report from Mayor Dave Bing's office.

Dangerous? Deadly? Poor? Impoverished? Who knew as an adolescent that these adjectives were the depiction of a place I called "Home Sweet Home"? I can still smell the sweet and sour fragrance reeking from 80% of the abandoned houses of my beggarly rich community full of people living in their comfortable misery. As the youngest of 4 boys to a single parent mother, not having role models, goals or any inspiration to combat the systemic oppression inflicted on our impoverished neighborhood was the norm for me. Statistics reported that kids from this zip code will struggle with succeeding in elementary, middle and high school. Kids from this zip code are more likely to join a gang, experience drugs or engage in some violent activity at an early age. Kids from this zip code are less likely to receive a high school diploma and more likely to never obtain a college degree, have up to 3 kids by the age of 21 and by the age of 25 they will have been to jail at least once or dead!

Without a positive influence, my negative perspective on life led me to fall victim to most of these statistics. But before I adopted the morgue mentality of believing I would be better off dead than alive I had hope! I will never forget the warm, sunny day on Wednesday August 9, 2000. This was the day that I received my very first 100% on a work assignment in fourth grade. For the entire day, I had the biggest smile on my face because all I could think about was showing my mom how great of a job I did.

The hands on the clock struck 3 o'clock pm and I busted out of the doors of Marion Law Elementary and sprinted as fast as I could to the house. As I turned the corner onto our block, breathing profusely, my eyes were locked on my destination. The closer I got to my house the more peculiar the scenery became. A crowd of people who blocked my view of my house were crying and showing great signs of sorrow. After ambushing my way through the crowd there it was, all our belongings were laid out all over the yard and the street. My heart instantly dropped into my stomach as I watched my mother running in my direction, picking me up and saying, "Don't worry about this, Son, things will be okay".

I never got the chance to show my mother my 100%. I vividly remember, at 10 years of age, lifting my head up and sticking my chest out vowing to my mother that we will never go through this again but boy was I wrong. 48205 was not like any other neighborhood in Detroit Michigan, it was one that offered a variety of opportunities for innocent children like me. I will always remember what my big brother used to say about our neighborhood, "Welcome to the candy shop, Little Brother, but just be careful because all sales are final". I never understood what he meant, but, like most younger brothers, I was just happy to be in his presence, so I did not ask too many questions because of his quick temper. His catch phrase soon inspired my first entrepreneurial endeavor.

My mother worked 3 jobs (Manager at TJ Maxx, Assistant Manager at Rally's and Retail Clerk at Ashley Stewart) to provide for the 4 of us. I never got to see her much, but I knew she was checking on us because every morning we would wake up to the wonderful smell of Triple Big Buford's, large fries and Cokes from Checkers every morning that were to hold us over until dinner. Alongside the food was $80; my oldest brother would hand each of us $20 and say, "This is your bus fare for the entire week".

Now, after the $1.50 plus $0.25 transfer to and from school the total amount would equal up to $17.50, leaving me with $2.50 of spending money for the entire week. On this budget, I learned how to lose my appetite so that I did not get sick for being hungry throughout the day. I learned how to ignore my peripheral vision when I saw other kids in the cafeteria line on Mondays and Wednesdays when they served BBQ chicken wings. I learned how to downplay football and basketball camps that were being offered because I knew that with $2.50 I probably could not afford the flyer they were passing out. Although I played a role through so many instances I knew I was lying to myself about enjoying being poor. Living in 48205 with the "Have Nots" I knew I had to find a way to make more money so that I could buy things like chips, juice, NOW and LATER's and chicken wings on Monday and Wednesdays. You know the luxury things in life that all kids yearn for at the age of 11, LOL.

So, after riding the Detroit Department of Transportation (DDOT) buses to and from school, starting at one location, getting off to catch another bus then walking 3 blocks to arrive at home for weeks, my master plan started to form in my head. Why not serve a product that I could get for cheap, get to and from school and transfer the product into a container that was easily accessible anywhere that would make profit? It's funny how observing my route on the DDOT bus inspired my very first entrepreneurial endeavor. Even though I had an idea of the service, I had no clue as to what the product would be. Being the youngest child, I was the most observant. I watched my brothers do almost everything from brushing their teeth in the morning to what side of the bunk bed they would sleep on. My brothers were always so cool to me, so the smallest things that they did had the biggest impact on me.

One day, my brother, Antonio, was making what is known to be one of the "Top Shelf" drinks in most impoverished communities, Kool-Aid. He ripped off the top of the Kool-Aid packet and the vapors rising into the sky caused my eyes to light up! He then poured the Kool-Aid into the container that was three fourths filled with water and stirred. My head started moving in a circular motion as I was hypnotized by the elegant way of how he stirred it. He then added the final ingredient, which was sugar, and I watched it flow down to the bottom of the container and I asked him, "Bro, why does the sugar go straight to the bottom instead of floating around in the water?".

He responded, "Sugar has more density than the water. Always remain solid in life, Little Bro, that way you will also have a strong foundation, and nothing can knock you off your square". My brother always had an analogy for things which made him so cool to me. After this 5-minute conversation, my master plan hit me. I told myself I would start selling Kool-Aid packages without the water (because I wanted to have a solid foundation just like my big brother taught me). So, I began to do the numbers, which came out to be 20 Kool-Aid packets for $1.06 and 1 bag of sugar for $1.59 totaling out to be $2.65. My first question was, *"How am I going to get the $0.15 to purchase the product?"*. My next question was, *"Without a container how can I market my product?"*. I did not want to ask one of my brothers for $0.15 because we only had $2.50 of spending money for the entire week. So, I made a proposal to all 3 of my brothers that if each one of them loaned me $0.05 I would give them $0.25 within a week. I figured I would be generous for their investment into my first business.

Now that my first problem had been handled and my next issue was getting containers to market my product. After removing my Kool-Aid packets and sugar from the grocery bag, in that moment; my idea was complete! *If I use grocery bags I can make them in different sizes and sell them for $0.25, $0.50 and $1.00.* I began the manufacturing portion of the process. I took the pitcher that my brother used to make Kool-Aid, washed it and dried it very well. I poured the entire bag of sugar into the container and then I ripped open the Kool-Aid packets, amazed at the vapor flowing into the air, then I poured them on top of the sugar. After I stirred up the Kool-Aid mix, I poured the different portions into the grocery bags and stuffed them into my book bag. As I laid down that night all I could think about was everybody running up to me with money in their hands trying to purchase my product.

I woke up early the next morning because this day was the beginning of me making hundreds of dollars (well, at least I thought I was, LOL). I went through the normal routine I had been going through all week, waking up to the smell of Triple Big Buford's, large fries and Cokes, hopping on the bus and getting my transfer and then observing the entire ride until I reached my destination.

Walking in the doors of Barbara Magnet Middle School on October 15, 2002 I felt like a new man. I walked up to all the students who stood at the most popular location in the school said the phrase, "Welcome to the Candy Shop!". As I opened my book bag and pulled out the product, students started running up to me like I was passing out A+ for report cards. By the third hour the entire school knew that I was selling Kool-Aid and wanted to invest in my business. The only problem was that I ran out of product. With so much demand and little supply I started to wonder, *"How can I expand my inventory to avoid running into this issue ever again?"*. After one day of business, I had turned my $2.65 investment into $22.50 with a $19.85 profit.

After my last hour of school, my brothers and I linked up so that we could catch the DDOT bus home and they noticed a huge smile on my face. "What's up with you, Bro?" Deon asked.

I said "You 'll see as soon as I get home", with a little chuckle.

I knew not to pull out money in public because there would be a great chance that by the time we got off the DDOT bus someone would have taken it from me. Once my brothers and I got home, I asked them all to come into the front room and said, "I know I promised you all $0.25 by the end of the week, but because business is doing so good payday came a few days early". As I pulled out the $22.50 I could see the eyes of my brothers growing in awe.

"How did you make all of that money?" Leon asked.

Then I told them about my business and they were all proud of me. I went to the grocery store to purchase more inventory so that I could be more prepared for tomorrow. With more money, I could acquire more flavors to add variety to my products.

When I arrived at school the next day, I noticed a crowd of students surrounding my locker. I heard a student ask, "When will the candy shop be open?". After the first hour, I had already made $9.25, and at that point, I had projected to surpass the proceeds from the previous day. Then my first flaw in my product was revealed to me. An angry customer informed me that all their Kool-Aid had fallen into their pocket out of the grocery bag and he felt like I needed to provide him with another bag free of charge.

Now like any other business person, I knew that giving away free merchandise was never good for business, but I did not want a bad rumor to spread, so I apologized and gave him a bigger bag of Kool-Aid on the house. I thought of a quick fix to avoid this from happening to anyone else. I went to one of my favorite teachers, Mrs. Denise Brown, with a proposition. I proposed that if she allowed me a box of safety clips a week for my business I would help her grade papers throughout the week. I remembered overhearing her say to another teacher that she could use some help a couple weeks ago. She agreed and handed me a box of 100 safety clips.

After the first week business was booming! I was bringing home an average of $25-$35 a day which allowed me to purchase all the junk food and BBQ chicken wings I wanted. I remember talking to my brother, Deon, and he made a comment that would soon take my business from good to great! He asked, "How come you call it the candy shop and only have one product?". At that moment, I knew it was time for expansion!

I went investigating around the grocery store to look for another product to sell and after spending 45 minutes of not finding anything, I began to get discouraged. As I was leaving the store, walking through the candy aisle, I saw the perfect product to add to my inventory - Frooties and NOW and LATER's!

Now, with various products, I almost tripled my profit daily, which made me a very happy kid in middle school. At this rate, I knew nothing could go wrong because I was living in paradise. Then it happened, the morning I woke up to with a different perspective.

CHAPTER 2: HIStory

The beauty of growing up in the struggle is that when you are younger, you do not view life as a struggle you just normalize the circumstances and indirectly inherit the impoverished mindset that comes with being poor. My creative mindset is a product of being a "Have Not". My surroundings forced me to imagine and dream of things that I knew I would never see or experience in life. I remember playing a game with my brothers called "Bingo". Whenever a nice car would pass us walking, we would call out, "Bingo!" to claim it. Even though we knew we would never sit in such a car, let alone drive it, the thought of it being ours was a wonderful feeling. Growing up with a lack of resources, one thought that lingers in your mind is how you can obtain more, so my brothers and I started another game called "Snatchies".

If any one of us had some food or candy that we wanted, we had full rights to snatch it right out of their hands. The only safety mechanism the person had was to call "No Snatchies", and then their belongings were off limits. This game was fun until someone snatched your food when you were hungry. It led me to acquiring habits that would lead me to a situation that I was not ready for.

On August 2, 2004, my cousin Timothy and I, decided to play Snatchies at the local grocery store. Ignoring the bubble gut feeling in my stomach and freezing hands from my nervousness, I knew I could not back out of this because I would get talked about by my cousin and friends. My cousin started on one end and I started on the other, stuffing our clothes with chips, candy and juice. Once we met up at our checkpoint we were ready to make a successful escape. Walking past the registers, I sensed a huge grin on my face knowing that I was about to feast on all of the stolen goods and then I heard a loud, "STOP! They're stealing".

Timothy took off and when you are from my neighborhood, the golden rule is when somebody takes off running, you follow suit. I started sprinting as fast as I could, bursting through the doors of the local grocery store. I crossed through traffic until I turned on my block and then I knew I was safe. After spending the next 10 minutes catching my breath, my cousin and I emptied out all our newly acquired treats.

"I knew they couldn't catch us, Cuz", Timothy said as he rambled through the snacks. Chips, cookies, oatmeal cakes, Frooties, SOUR PATCH's, Boston Baked Beans, SWISS ROLLS; you name it we had it. I felt bad for stealing from the local grocery store, but as soon as I bit into a SWISS ROLL, my feelings of sympathy were flushed out. Without my father or a male role model to discipline me, it was easy to do what I wanted without a care in the world.

Lying down, stuffed from eating junk food all day, I thought to myself, *"Today was a good day and I look forward to what tomorrow brings me"*.

"Get up, Bro, get up". I was being shaken awake by my brother.

Half asleep and confused, I asked, "Bro what's up? What's good? Why are you waking me up so early?".

"Pack your stuff, we have to be out of the house today", Deon replied.

Hearing those words was the smack in the face I needed to completely wake me up out of my sleep. "Why?" I asked Deon.

He said, "Bro we don't have time to talk about it, just pack and hurry up".

I found myself again in the position of feeling helpless and homeless. This eviction was different because not only were we getting put out again, we were getting split up. As the youngest child, I did not get told the details of everything, so I was confused as to why my brothers would have to live in two different places. Deon and I went to stay with my Aunt Roxanne and her 6 dependents, and Antonio and Leon went to stay with my cousin.

Antoine and Anthony, Roxanne two sons, became very close to Deon and I because we were all in the same age range. My aunt, who I call my second mom, was such a sweetheart. She welcomed my brother and I into her home with open arms and treated us the same as everyone else.

Being that we moved from one impoverished community to another, we adapted quickly. A habit that I picked up living with my cousins was smoking *Black and Mild's*. I had no idea what I was doing, but I wanted to fit in with everybody so that I did not become the outcast. After getting the hang of smoking, I decided to upgrade to smoking marijuana. Smoking became a way for me to step away from my circumstances and problems that I was dealing with in the world, so I fell in love with it.

As a freshman of Laura F. Osborn High School, my name held weight because all 3 of my older brothers went there. Inheriting the popularity from the path they had created made my high school career very fun and interesting. I made the Junior Varsity football team, which was a huge accomplishment for me and I could not wait to tell my mother. Every time I would accomplish anything, my mother was the first person to pop up in my head to tell. Not only did I make the football team, I made the basketball team, baseball team, got a 3.8 GPA and met one of my closest friends to this day, D'Andre Jackson.

Going into my sophomore year, I had a different perspective in life. I was the captain of both the football and basketball team, established a name for myself in school, all the ladies loved me even though I had a girlfriend and I had the highest GPA in my class. At this point in life nobody could tell me anything, I was Mr. Know it All. Every first hour, my brother and I would go into the bathroom where a few guys were always shooting dice. This was how I earned my money to do extracurricular things throughout the week. The crowd grew so big that the security guards picked up on the suspiciousness of us going in and not coming out until the end of the hour. We had to move the dice game every morning to a different location just to keep them from catching us. When the bell rang at the end of every hour, we had 5-10 minutes to get to our next class. Most students would linger around the most popular location call the "4 corners". Everything happened at the 4 corners; fights, transactions, conversations, etc.

I met another close friend by the name of Jose Anderson who was the class clown. The reason we became close was because I loved his personality. He was not afraid of being himself no matter what the circumstances were. During my sophomore year, I joined the National Honors Society and the robotics team, so my popularity continued to grow bigger and bigger.

One day, Jose and I were having a conversation in the back of our history class when our teacher, Mrs. White, asked us, "Would you two like to share with the entire class?".

My big mouth always got me in trouble, so I replied with "Sure since you seem interested". The entire class made a "oooh" sound at my response. "Why are we learning about this fake history? It's not black history so it ain't doing us no good", I said. Mrs. White said, "Well Mr. Clinton there aren't just black people in my class, so it wouldn't be fair to them if I didn't cover history as a whole, now would it?",

"Well, maybe we need segregation, Mrs. White", I responded. Once again, my big mouth was getting me into trouble.

"Leave the class, Mr. Clinton", Mrs. White demanded.

As I began packing up my things, Jose grabbed his belongings as well. As we were walking out of the class he turned around and said, "See you tomorrow", leaving the entire class in laughter.

The next day Mrs. White asked me to stay after class to talk about the incident from the previous day. "I don't know why you choose to act out Keyon; you are a very bright kid. It's okay to show how intelligent you are", she stated. This was the first time someone told me that I was very intelligent, and I felt as if they genuinely meant it. "What do you want to be 5 years from now?" she asked. "Alive", was my response.

"Well, be careful who you hang around with because the people you think are your friends can be the ones who bring you down in life", Mrs. White said.

In that moment, I felt a chill running through my body as if she was right. I never thought I was smart, even though I had a high GPA. I figured if you go to class and listen to the teacher the work should be easy. Undervaluing ourselves was normal in my neighborhood because there were no one around to reassure us that we were smart and could be successful in anything we put our minds to. When I went home to my aunt's that day, I remember talking to my mother on the phone and asking her, "Mom, why don't my father want to be here with us? Don't he know that his 4 sons need him?". "Life doesn't always go according to our plans, Keyon. Your father has his reasons for not being active in your life and when you and your father have a man-to-man conversation, I'm sure he'll explain to you why", my mother responded. One thing I always respected about my mother was the fact that I never heard her disrespect or antagonize the character of my father despite his absence in our lives.

My father was not 100% out of the picture, but being a sometime dad was not good enough for me. Even with the respectful response my mother gave me. I began to hate my father more and more each day for not being there. *"Who is supposed to teach me how to be a man?"* I thought to myself. My father did not teach me how to ride a bike, tie my shoes; or put on my clothes, so at this point, I decided I did not need him at all in my life.

Although there was hatred in my heart, I had learned to love the little things in life due to not having the luxuries of the rich kids. My aunt worked at a cleaner's company, so she would take our clothes to the cleaners so that we had clean clothes weekly. This was a relief because I remember days when we used the oven to heat the house at night and our clothes would smell like gas the next day.

High school was my safe space from all of life's reality. My popularity granted me access to things and areas that most students never got the chance to experience. From sitting in the principal's office talking about the student body to skipping class with the security guards made me feel like I was more privileged than the other students.

As I mentioned previously, I have always wanted to be like my big brothers and Deon was the brother I became closest to. They called me Little Deon my first two years of high school because we looked and acted alike. Basically, I was just mimicking his style. He played football, so I played football, he played baseball, so I played baseball, he was the most popular guy in school, so I wanted to be the most popular guy in school. With this much popularity comes attention and word was out that I was quite the ladies' man. When you're not used to this type of attention, it can become dangerous playing with women's hearts, which is what I did a lot. I was taught that I should never trust a woman and never to give her my love, so that was the mindset I had adopted until I saw her.

I remember walking up the hallway towards 4 corners with my best friend D'Andre Jackson when I tapped him and said, "Bro I need that in my life".

"Who Kyra?" D'Andre said.

"Uh yea, bro, who is that?".

"Bro, that's my girl twin sister".

Kyra Stafford, who was the twin of Kiara Stafford had the most beautiful and innocent face that I had ever seen. I couldn't help but notice her caramel tone skin and voluptuous body. In that moment, I just knew I had found the one. After introducing myself and flattering her with my sweet nothings I knew she would soon be all mine. I mean I did win class flirt for a reason. After spending countless hours of conversing on the phone and enjoying each other's presence after my football practices every day, I decided to make her my very first girlfriend. She was inspired by all the things I was a part of, which made her get active in extracurricular activities such as basketball, softball and supporting my robotics team. Throughout all the time I invested in her I could feel my love growing stronger and stronger, but not even love could stop my desires from feeding on the attention from other women. The popularity got to my head and I started to feel invincible. I messed around with multiple women behind Kyra's back, but I just knew that I was too smart to get caught until someone else caught feelings for me.

When Kyra found out that I cheated on her, it broke my heart. *"How could I hurt someone I truly love?"* I asked myself. It reminded me of all the men who came in and out of my mother's life, leaving her with a broken heart, including my father. *"Am I becoming my father?"* I asked myself. After a while of being in my feelings I would justify my actions by thinking that nobody had ever taught me how to love so I was supposed to make mistakes; another mask that I would put on to disguise the ugly truths of my life.

I remember going home to my aunt's house and seeing a bunch of candles and push-on wall lamps in grocery bags. "Aunt Roxy, what are all these candles for?" I asked. "The lights and gas are cut off", she responded.

Even though I had experienced this a plethora of times in my life the feeling of my heart falling in my stomach remained the same. I could feel myself going back to the sunken place of giving up and accepting the fact that I would be poor forever.

Antoine, Anthony, Deon and I went to the gas station to get out the house and enjoy the few moments of sunlight we had left until we had to light candles to see in the house. "Bro, do you think our life is cursed?" I asked Deon.

"Naw, Bro, we can't control what happens to us, all we can do is accept it and find a way to move forward". My brother was always optimistic about our living situations and for some reason I had absolutely no idea why. I felt like we were living in hell. "Besides, Key, we have been through this multiple times, it can't get any worse", Deon added. Although I did not believe in the words that my brother told me, he was the only person in the world that I trusted, so I gave him the benefit of the doubt.

All four of us sat on the front porch joking and laughing while eating the snacks we got from the gas station. After eating a big bag of Hot Cheetos, I needed to quench my thirst with a cold glass of water because my mouth was burning. I was very precise with how many ice cubes that I used for my water. I needed 4 ice cubes every time for the right temperature. I grabbed my cup, put in 4 ice cubes and stuck my cup under the faucet and twisted the knob. Nothing happened! The last thing you need to happen when your mouth is on fire is not to have anything to drink afterwards. I twisted the knob again to make sure I was not hallucinating. I ran outside and said, "Cuz, the kitchen sink is broke".

"What? Cuz, you tripping. It ain't nothing wrong with the sink", Antoine responded.

After he came in and turned the knob he realized that I was serious. "Ma! Come help us!" Antoine yelled to my aunt Roxy.

"Boy what's the matter?" she asked.

"The sink is not working", Antoine said.

"Damn, the water is off too", aunt Roxy said.

After sucking on ice cubes to chill my mouth from burning, I finally felt relieved. All I could think about were my brother's words telling me that things could not get any worse, but boy was he wrong. With no water, lights or gas how could one survive through this madness. We could not cook food, wash clothes or watch television. I felt like I was literally living in a prison, but the inmates had a better life than I did now. *"How could a bad situation get worse in a matter of hours?"* I thought to myself. *"This must be the lowest point of my life and it's only up from here"*, I told myself after thinking about my brother's optimism.

Then my stomach grumbled. After eating junk food all day, it finally caught up with me. I had to release this waste that was causing my stomach to bubble but then it hit me that we did not have any water, so the toilet would not flush.

"Aunt Roxy, I have to use the bathroom", I told her.

"Go in the back and pee by the alley", she responded.

"But I don't have to pee Aunt" I said while I could feel my stomach getting weaker and weaker from holding it in and squeezing my butt together.

"Here, take this grocery bag and some tissue and go in the back", Aunt Roxy said. After experiencing having to use the bathroom outside in a grocery bag I did not even feel human.

Before I went to sleep that night realizing that this was one of the worst days in my life, I told God "Whatever it is you're punishing me for you have made your point. I'm sorry".

Life was such a blur at this point. I was just going through the motions at school; I lost interest in extracurricular activities, I started to get used to living with no water, lights and gas and I had lost hope of anything positive happening in the life of Keyon Clinton.

It had been a few weeks since the last time my mother and I talked, and she called my aunt to speak to me. I was excited because she told me she was bringing my favorite Triple Big Buford, large Rally fries and a Coke in the morning. I was yearning for the morning to have a good meal and see my mother because I missed her so much. That night was different when I laid down because I had something to look forward to in the morning, so I went to sleep as optimistic as I could be. Then I woke up to an awkward smell.

CHAPTER 3: WHAT GOES UP MUST COME DOWN

I vividly remember waking up to my mom and brother having a conversation and her saying to him, "I don't know what happened". I ran into the front room looking around and wondering why I did not smell the Triple Big Buford's and Rally fries that my nose was accustomed to; but instead I saw the same tears and face full of sorrow that I'd seen on August 9, 2000.

I had to ask my mother, "Mom are we getting put out again?". She informed me that she got fired from Rally's and laid off from TJ Maxx in the same week; not knowing where we would get the funds to help pay rent.

As I mentioned before, 48205 was not like any other neighborhood in Detroit, Michigan; it was one that offered a variety of opportunities for innocent children like me. After discussing this tragic news with a cousin who I knew made a lot of money from his profession, he introduced me to a game that I found myself getting attached to quickly. After a week of selling weed and seeing the profit I made from it, I knew my days of selling Kool-Aid and candy were over. At first, I was doing it to help provide rent for my mother, and the more successful I became at it; the more I started to love the game and all the perks that came with it. I became my cousin's right-hand man and he introduced me to his circle. I fell in love with the fast money, fast life, jewelry, women and rep that I was getting, but little did I know that there are no brakes in the fast lane.

I started developing the mindset that by any means necessary I had to get my next dollar, so I started taking the things I wanted. I told my mother I had a job so that she would not become suspicious of this random money that I had coming in,9 but the more I hung around my cousin the more questions she asked me about my location and activities while I was out.

In any job in the world, hard work will always be rewarded. I was appointed leader of a specific crew of an area in my neighborhood because of the hard work and dedication that I exuded in the streets. They called me "Beans", a reference from state property because of my "get down or lay down" mentality. I did not take anything from anyone and I was loyal to my team. My crew and I did everything together. We ate, hung out, spent time and essentially became a brotherhood with a bond that could not be broken. For the first time in my life I felt like I was in control of things. I approached the streets with the same mindset I had in middle school when I was selling candy. I would walk on the block and say, "Welcome to the Candy

Shop! Where all sales are final". It was in that moment that I finally understood exactly what my brother meant with that statement.

I was so rooted in the game I felt like there was no return. I may never know what it feels like to be the President of the United States of America, but I do know what it feels like to be the head person in charge of a certain group. All transactions went through my approval; I had my crew reporting to me every night, setting up plans for expansion and taking over territories. I grew up watching my favorite movie of all time *"PAID IN FULL"* and it was interesting because I felt like Ace in the cleaners wanting to live a good, humble life but the streets called me, and I had to answer. One of my OG's used to always tell me, "Everything that glitters isn't gold. Watch every step you take". I had no thought in my mind that anyone on my team would cross me or jeopardize our operation but boy was I wrong.

When an operation is working successfully, and everybody is getting money, you would think that the entire team would be happy, but that was not the case here. A member of the crew wanted more power in the way things were being organized and operated. Once I told him no, I could sense a different vibe every time he came around us. I started to see new faces on the block, which made me a little skeptical. New business does not mean that it's good for business in this profession. I kept my cool and continued operating the Candy Shop.

On the beautiful morning of June 17, 2006, I remember riding with my second-in-command to pick up inventory for the Candy Shop operation. The entire time I was asking him about whether he had noticed the new people and how he felt about the recent behavior of our envious crew member. He said he'd noticed the new faces but reminded me that our goal was to expand so he did not think anything of it. He proceeded to inform me that it might be best to remove the envious crew member before things escalated to something we both did not want it to go to. I knew I had to make an executive decision to remove him.

When we arrived at the location, the scenery was a little peculiar. The distributor was not there, and he was never late because he understood that time is money. Before I could call to find out what was the reason for the no show, I saw two guys approach both sides of the car with pistols pointed at us. My heart was pounding through my chest and I could feel my stomach sinking, trying to gasp for air. This was my first time ever in a situation where my life flashed before my eyes.

I heard the deep voice of the man utter, "Where is the money?".

"What money?" my second-in-command asked.

The man with the deep voice uttered, "this is your last chance!".

With my back facing them I had no idea what was going on over there and then I heard a sound that will forever play in the back of my head. I heard a loud boom and a vicious scream from my second-in-command; at that moment I knew he was shot. Now my legs were shaking uncontrollably because I knew I was next.

The deep voice uttered, "get the money now!".

Once they got the money from the back seat the other voice asked, "Should we kill him too?".

The man with the deep voice responded with, "Let him live, his life ain't worth shit anyway".

45

Hearing the skidding rubber from their tires as they drove off still makes my ears cringe until this day when I see or hear cars burning rubber.

I ran over to check on my second-in-command only to find him taking his last breaths. "Be strong, bro, don't die on me, I need you!" was all I could say while seeing the blood pour out of his body like a fountain. He held me tight and whispered, "Tell my mom I love her", as his eyes closed for the last time.

In that moment, not only did I lose my second in command, I lost all my feelings for people. My heart grew cold and I wanted revenge. I met up with my cousin the next day to discuss what happened and I mentioned that I believed my envious crew member had something to do with it. Word spreaded fast in our neighborhood and everybody knew I was looking for revenge. The colder my heart grew the less I trusted anyone, causing me to engage in some activities that I will forever take to my grave. Speaking of graves, I had officially adopted the "morgue mentality".

We were at war in the street with a rival crew, so the streets became dry, the money slowed up and that fast life did not seem to be so fast anymore. Being a leader of a crew is great until everybody starts questioning your moves; "What are we gone do?", "Have you made any more connects? Because I need this money", "You told us you got us through anything, so what you got Beans?". I was in an uncomfortable position because I had just lost a close friend and all everybody cared about was making the next dollar.

When I went home that night, I laid on the bed and did a self-assessment of my life. That was the first time I thought about leaving the game and starting a new life, but I realized that I was in too deep. Then a voice in my head said, *"Well, look at the bright side, this is as worse as it gets so it's only up from here"*. I psyched myself into believing that my days would get better in this game, but boy was I wrong again.

My cousin, who went to school to become a lawyer did not finish because he was a product of his environment and could not adjust to college; he did not receive his degree, but he gained a massive amount of knowledge in the law field. He's been to court a plethora of times with no representation because he knew the law so well. When you are living with two strikes on your record it does not matter how well you know law when a judge declares that if he ever sees your face inside of the courtroom again you will never see daylight again.

On Thanksgiving November 22, 2007, my cousin pulled me to one side at my aunt's house and said, "Cuz we 'bout to go get some new cars, you down?". Of course, they were not talking about going to the dealership to finance a new lease, so I decided to sit this trip out because I wanted to spend time with the family. Two days later, I realized that I had not heard from my cuz, which was weird, so I rode around the city to find him, but there was no word from anybody.

Three days later, on a beautiful Sunday, November 25, 2007, around 3:00 p.m. I was sitting in the living room watching my favorite movie *PAIN IN FULL*, which was my normal routine every Sunday. In the middle of my favorite part of the movie, I remember the front door getting kicked in. "Freeze!", was the only thing I heard from the officers.

Fully automatic weapons pointed at the back of my head while my face was mushed into the living room floor. The only thought going through my head was, *"What the hell did I do?"*. My mother rushed down stairs screaming, "Stop! Keyon, what did you do?". What did you do?".

The officer informed my mom that I was under arrest for armed robbery. The look of disappointment on my mother's face as the cop car pulled off pierced my heart like never before.

I remember the 20-minute ride to the police department feeling like 2 hours. I arrived at the police department still confused because I did not perform any armed robbery, so I needed answers and fast. After 5 hours of sitting in a cold cell with my head down, assessing all the mistakes I had made since joining the game and praying to God about giving me another chance and forgiving me for my sins, I heard the doors opening.

"Keyon Clinton", the officer called out.

"Yes sir", I replied.

"Come with me. Looks like you are free to go". I looked up in the sky because I never knew God was listening to my prayers until this moment. I got to the front counter to retrieve my belongings and the officer informed me that the guy they were looking for was forging my name for all his offenses, but ironically, he used the name Kenyon Clinton. I asked for the name of the person who had been framing me this whole time and come to find out it was my cousin. My heart fell in my stomach.

"How could he do this to me?", was all I could think about. This was the man who introduced me to the game, who gave me my first product and brought me into his operation. *"I thought he loved and cared about me"*, was the other thought going through my head as I was escorted home by my mother.

"See, Keyon I knew you had no right being with him in the first place". My mother continued to harp on the situation the entire ride home about my brothers' and my safety and how our decisions affect more than just ourselves. At the time, I was in such distress that I could not comprehend a word she was saying.

Growing up in my neighborhood, you learned how to bottle up your emotions quickly but this night I cried like a baby. I never would have thought that the one guy who I knew I could trust was using me as bait to keep himself out of trouble. Waking up the next morning I knew I had to leave the game completely because the only options were jail time or death and I did not want either choice.

I was able to get the court date for my cousin and decided to go just so I could see his face one more time before he got sentenced. Before walking in the courtroom, I had to take a deep breath and remind myself not to snap and keep my composure. I remember hearing the judge ask my cousin, "So what do you have to say for yourself?" and hearing my cousin intelligently giving a heartwarming plea for sympathy for his mistakes.

The judge took a deep breath and said, "I remember telling you the last time that if I saw you in here that you would be put away for a long time" and sentenced him to 40 years in prison.

Life has its own way of showing you how your actions can have major consequences and seeing my cousin get 40 years in prison was a huge reality check for me. As they hand cuffed him and escorted him out of the court room, he looked me in the eyes with tears dripping down his face saying, "I'm so sorry, Cuz, I'm so sorry".

They say there are no brakes in the fast lane, but they don't say that you can't jump out of the car. In that moment, I left the game and everything that came with it on the seat in the court room. Walking out of that court room, I felt like I was leaving behind everything that I had owned, so my only question to myself was, "Was it all worth it?".

CHAPTER 4: VICTIM OR VICTOR?

I used to always think to myself, *"Why would God place me in such a crippling situation in life?"*. *"I didn't ask for this God, why me?"*. Then I came across a few Bible verses that changed my perspective: whenever I questioned if I was a mistake or not I would read Isaiah 44:2 (NLT). "The Lord who made you and helps you says: O dear Israel, my chosen one". When I thought about why God allowed me to be born into poverty I would read Acts 17:26 (NIV). The Bible says, "From one man he made every nation and he determined the times set for them and the exact places where they should live". Times when I felt I was in pure darkness and could not see any light at the end of the tunnel I would read Matthew 5:14-16 (NLT). "You are the light of the world, like a city on a hilltop that cannot be hidden. No one lights a lamp and then puts it under a basket. Instead, a lamp is placed on a stand, where it gives light to everyone in the house. In the same way, let your good deeds shine out for all to see, so that everyone will praise your heavenly Father". Then when I questioned my ability to be great because I could not see greatness within myself I read these two verses: Psalm 139:15 (NLT). "You watched me as I was being formed in the utter seclusion, as I was woven together in the dark of the womb" and Psalm 238:8 (NLT) "The LORD will work out his plans for my life – for your faithful love, O LORD, endures forever. Don't abandon me, for you made me".

I was forced to go to church when I was younger by my aunt Tara and I hated it because I was too young to even understand what church and God meant. I thought the people were delusional, worshipping something they couldn't see or hear. The longer I stayed and prayed; the more God started revealing himself to me and showing me things that ensured his existence and truths of the Bible. I began thinking about some things to change my perspective on life. The Bible says that my birth was no mistake or mishap, and my life is no fluke of nature. Even if my parents did not plan to have me, God did, and he was not surprised by my birth, he expected it. So, my life does have meaning to it and I do belong here, but why? God also planned where I would be born and where I would live for his purpose. Being black was intentional by him. God left no detail to chance. He planned it all for his purpose. So, God strategically placed me in an impoverished community to endure the struggles of life that I faced.

Most amazingly, God decided how I would be born. Regardless of the circumstances of my birth or who my parents are, God had a plan in creating me. It doesn't matter whether my parents were good, bad, or indifferent; God knew that those two individuals possessed exactly the right genetic makeup to create me in his image. They had the DNA God wanted to make me. While there are illegitimate parents, there are no illegitimate children. Many children are unplanned by their parents, but they are not unplanned by God. God's purpose considered human error, and even sin, but why? For so long I had lived in a dark place in my life, through evictions, rejections, depression, oppressions, mass incarcerations and societal disadvantages due to my race and gender. *"How can anyone see light when there is a dark cloud following them everywhere they go?"*, I thought. Matthew 5:14-16 taught me that I was in a dark place because I had not found the light within myself. All this time I had been waiting on someone, or something, to shed light on my situation instead of just flicking on the switch within me. I had no clue how I could find this gift that was shining so bright within me and shed light on everyone else in my life like the Bible said, but I had always endeavored to find out. God had chosen me to be a light to the world but why? Psalm 139:15 explained to me that God prescribed every single detail of my body. He deliberately chose my race, the color of my skin, my hair, and every other feature. He custom-made my body just the way he wanted it. He also determined the natural talents that I would possess and the uniqueness of my personality. Psalm 138:9 simply explained that, long before I was conceived by my parents, I was conceived in the mind of God. It is not fate, chance, luck, or coincidence that I am breathing at this very moment. I am alive because God wanted to create me! The LORD will fulfill his purpose for me. These Bible verses helped me gain clarity on the confusion as to why I was alive, why I kept experiencing all of this trauma. Why didn't my father want his children? Would I ever live a positive and healthy lifestyle? Most importantly, it changed my perspective from playing the victim to appreciating the hard times because it built me into a more tenacious and ambitious teenager with a mental fortitude that could withstand the hardest blows of life.

Changing my mindset and perspective was a difficult task for me because I possessed negative habits that would land me back at square one and my environment was a constant reminder that I was never meant to be anything in life other than a stupid, drug dealing criminal who belonged in jail or dead. To combat these statistics and stereotypes, I posted my favorite Bible scriptures on the wall and I would review them every day and night until I felt better about myself. "No longer will I use my oppressions as an excuse as to why I will not be successful in life", is a statement I said to myself every day my senior year of high school.

Entering my senior year of high school, I had the perfect path any student could imagine. I had a 3.8GPA, I was the captain of the football, baseball and robotics team, I was the most popular guy in school, the ladies loved me, and I stayed in the latest gear, so I knew that this year was going to be a breeze. By this time, I was living back with my mother and we were in a position to maintain the normality of living in poverty.

Although everybody used to tell me that I was so smart, I never believed I was. I thought if you just listened to the teacher, you would understand the material. No one instilled confidence in me so the only thing I knew was to doubt myself and devalue my worth. If there was one person who believed in me when I was in high school other than my brother Deon, it was Coach Coker. Coach Coker was the lifeline of Laura F. Osborn High School. He was a father to some, an uncle, brother, coach, mentor, etc., but to me he was truly an angel sent from heaven. He coached all three of my older brothers at Osborn, so he knew me before I even got there, and he treated me just like family since day one of my freshman year. He would always tell me, "Keyon, you have the content, but you don't have the character".

"Coach what you mean? I got good grades, I'm the man, I take care of myself. You can't tell me nothing coach", was always my response. Then, one day, he sat me in his office and told me these words that changed my perspective forever. He said, "Keyon, character is doing the right thing because it is the right thing to do. Not when people are looking, not when the cameras are on but simply because your heart is in the right place". I felt those words pierce through my heart like a sharp blade. I could not get those words out of my head. Even to this day I can still hear his voice in my head whenever I am about to make a bad decision. The Lord works in Godly ways because, with my brother Deon being in college, I felt alone a lot, so the fact that I could trust Coach Coker, that helped me get through high school.

Whenever I would pray for patience, it seemed as if God would bring something in my life to irritate me. Things were starting to incline in my life, so I knew that, with my temper, I would need patience on this journey. I missed having a brotherhood when I was younger, so I joined a gang called "The Goodfellas". They were becoming my new family. I thought I learned from my previous mistakes not to hang around the wrong people, but for some reason I just knew this time it was different. I loved the fact that we would always greet each other with a special handshake, two claps and a salute. Our leader was so well respected that whoever was affiliated with the gang received a certain level of respect. Being the youngest and smallest brother, I always had to fight to prove my realness to people. Being a front-line soldier earned me the nickname "BEANS" when I got introduced to the game and I upheld that title even with the Goodfellas.

I was the epitome of the saying, "You are who you hang around", because even though I wanted better for my life, I could not resist fighting, stealing and doing regretful things with my gang brothers simply because it was their norm and I wanted to fit in. When the leader went to prison, the Goodfellas movement came to a halt. Seeing that our plan was to take from other people and businesses to get the bond money made me uncomfortable; in that moment, I knew I wanted out. Through all the attempts we made to acquire the bond money, we came up short and our risks were becoming more dangerous with every attempt. One day, I just told my brother, "I cannot do this anymore because I have already been down this road and I know what two destinations are ahead of us". After that conversation, I left the group and never looked back.

Being able to walk away from fast money, rental cars and girls made me realize that I was changing on the inside. Although it was tough to leave the gang of men I called brothers, it hurt me the most being called soft, weak and a pussy by some of them. I just knew that I was making the right decision even though I wanted to fight to prove my realness again. "Lord, am I making the right decision? Do I need to be in a group of men that I think will protect me even though we're living wrong? Am I soft?" These were some of the questions that I would ask God because I was so confused as to what my next steps would be in life after my decision to leave the gang.

Then I came across four Bible verses in Proverbs that gave me clarity for my future. Proverbs 3:5-6, "Trust in the LORD with all your heart and lean not on your own understanding; in all your ways submit to him, and he will make your paths straight". Proverbs 19:20-21, "Listen to advice and accept discipline, and at the end you will be counted among the wise. Many are the plans in a person's heart, but it is the LORD's purpose that prevails". Then it finally hit me that everything that I was the victim of taught me how to maneuver through future adversity so that I could come out victorious. It was in that moment I believed that

God was about to reveal some things to me. Boy, was I right!

PHASE 2: REVELATION

CHAPTER 5: HEALING THE LIVING DEAD

At the age of 16, I did not have a care in the world. My heart was cold, and I was numb to caring about people's feelings. I had adopted the "Morgue" mentality. I was physically alive but mentally and morally dead. I was going through life with no purpose or agenda. Honestly, I did not care whether I lived or died. The truth is that a lot of people are living a life without purpose. Before you can find your purpose, you must first find yourself. I would always blame everybody else for the circumstances I was placed in. I blamed my parents for not being successful in life; I blamed my brothers for not always showing me the way as the youngest; I blamed my schools for not giving me the best education and I blamed my environment for the bad decisions that I had made in life. I had no clue what my purpose in life was, so I was easily influenced by the things that surrounded me. The answer to finding your true purpose is life in found in the Bible verse Matthew 6:33 "But seek first his kingdom and his righteousness and all these things will be given to you as well".

I am a firm believer that, for those who truly seek after God, he will provide you with clarity on your assignment in life and he will provide you with the necessary tools for your journey.

When I stopped blaming others and began looking in the mirror and faced myself, I gained a new perspective in life. The revelation I received from God was real. He showed me during this process that life was not about me. We are blessed to be a blessing to other people. All the people who were close to me needed me to impact and support them in ways that they could not support themselves. As good as this sounded, the truth was that I was a very selfish individual at the time. I struggled with humbling myself to do what God wanted me to do and serve people because of my current circumstance. "How do you expect me to give to people when I don't have anything?", I asked God. I come from a background of poverty, struggle, selfishness, hate, crime and no love, so there was no way I could see myself being anything different than what I was used to.

Whenever I would struggle with God's request for my life, I would go to him in prayer. "God, give me a word for understanding because I don't have much to offer the world", I prayed. I felt like I had little to no value in this world so why waste my energy trying to convince others to be great and successful when I did not even believe that I could be great and successful?

In my dream one night, God placed Genesis 1:26 on my heart and I woke up and read it. Then God said, "Let us make mankind in our image, in our likeness, so that they may rule over the fish in the sea and the birds in the sky, over the livestock and all the wild animals, and over all the creatures that move along the ground." In reading that I took away that I have dominion over the earth and that the world is mine. Although I had good intentions, my execution was not always good with this thought. I walked around feeling like I could do and say whatever I wanted because the world was mine. Misinterpreting this verse got me in a lot of trouble.

I started paying closer attention to my surroundings. I had friends who only wanted to be around when it benefitted them. I started watching how people would use my mom because she has a giving spirit. Most importantly, I started to watch my habit of how I would say I was tired of the struggle but still placed myself in the same situations that kept me in that state of mind. A part of me wanted to live right and see where that life took me, but the other part of me was so consumed with this lifestyle I just could not see a way out. *"How many times do you have to bump your head to get it, Keyon?"*, I asked myself. In life, we pray for signs and when God sends them to us we tend to act as if we are unsure if they came from him. What I have learned is that when you ask God for things, you may not always like the sacrifices you have to make or the way that he goes about giving them to you.

Walking around with this mindset of not caring whether I lived or died made me very impulsive with my ideas. I stayed fighting, stealing, short cutting and taking the easy route to temporary satisfaction because I had no vision of longevity in life. I asked God to show me my enemies and a couple close friends and I started falling out. I asked God to help me grow as a man and he sent down rain over my life. I had a problem with taking things that did not belong to me, so I asked God to remove that habit. I remember how we used to steal so much out of the gas station we stopped being discreet about it. The clerk knew why we were coming in every day but was too afraid to stop us.

One day, I went in there alone and grabbed a box of Little Debbie Oatmeal Creme Pies and he was prepared. When I went to the back, I did not see the clerk come from behind the glass. I began to make my escape and there he was standing at the door with his 9mm handgun pointed in my direction. "Stop!", he yelled. I felt my heart drop in my stomach as I anticipated him pulling the trigger. "Why do you come here and steal from me every day? I'm calling the police", he continued, yelling at me.

"It won't be smart to call the cops. You don't want to have to deal with my people every day. Just let me go and I won't come back here again. Trust me, you don't want these problems", I threatened the clerk.

"Just go and don't come back", he yelled in his Chaldean accent.

Later I realized that God allowed me to go through that situation to understand why I needed to stop stealing. From that moment forward, I vowed never to steal from that gas station again. The more I was exposed to, the more I realized that mentally and morally I was living wrong. I could never reach success, happiness or fame if I continued to live wrong and not appreciate life. I was the living dead. I had no purpose in life and, because I felt inferior, I would do anything to make me feel superior to others. I lacked exposure and that is why I struggled with shaking off those bad habits. I wanted to do better, and I thought about living a better life, but my reality was crushing my hopes and dreams living in poverty every day.

A lot of people struggle with shifting paradigms within them because of their lack of exposure. Having dreams and visions are great, but that is only 2D. Being exposed to something greater is more 3D and attainable. For example, I never believed I could play baseball because I watched it on TV and I did not think I had the ability to play although I envisioned myself being on the field. When I finally made the decision to try out and made the team, I began believing in myself even before playing my first game. I did not have the resources to get exposed to things, so I started asking my teachers, coaches and older neighbors to teach me things that I did not know. As my perspective began to change, I felt a shift in my thinking and actions. The two most important days in your life are the day you were born and the day you figure out your purpose. Nothing was going to stop me from figuring out my purpose in life. I knew that something needed to happen for me to snap out of my way of thinking but I could not wrap my mind around what it would be. Little did I know that I would receive my revelation sooner than I thought.

HEALING THE LIVING DEAD

<u>CHAPTER 6: THE WAKE-UP CALL</u>

It was the day that every senior yearned for in high school. Today was Senior Skip Day. On this day, all the seniors skipped class to meet at the secret location and partake in some festivities that only the students could speak of. I woke up with a different smile on this day knowing I was going to be skipping school as if I had not been skipping class my entire high school career. Today, skipping class just seemed more acceptable by the school.

I arrived at school and met with the seniors to discuss the secret location and time that we were going to meet up when I realized I left my identification card at home. Usually I would get irritated when I made silly mistakes, but nothing could steal my joy because today was a special day. Walking up to my house I was startled to see my mother's brown Sable in the driveway. *"Shouldn't she be at work?"*, I asked myself. I sat outside for about 10 minutes trying to come up with a lie to explain why I was not in class. When I got my story straight, I walked in the house quietly and my mom was not in sight. I tip-toed to my room to grab my identification card and began to tip-toe towards the front door. Once I reached the door, I heard my mother crying. As I walked up the stairs carefully, trying not to get caught by the obnoxious squeaking noise of the wooden steps, I overhead her talking to an anonymous person.

"I can't take it anymore", she said. "I am sick of living like this. I'm working 3 jobs, living check to check and I can barely provide for my children". "My sons don't have a male role model and I just know that they are going to get killed in these streets". "I'm just ready to pick up all my things and run away". I couldn't take anymore words from the conversation, so I left the house.

My heart was filled with so many emotions after hearing this conversation that my mother was having. I was sad because my mom was my superman and to know that she was hurting was hurting me. I was angry because I was not able to help provide so that we could live a better life. I was confused because I couldn't figure out why God was punishing my family. My face full of tears, I sat on the bench at the local park around the corner from my house. *"How could I cause pain to one of the people I love the most?"*, I asked myself. In that moment, I realized how my decisions and actions affected other people who cared about me. After releasing my emotions, I wiped away my tears and said, "It's time for a change".

Two things that never happened were that I never told my mom, even to this day, about the conversation I overheard, and I never made it to Senior Skip Day. The next day I was bombarded by classmates asking, "Where were you?" and "Is everything okay?".

"Yea I'm good, I had a family emergency", was my response.

I was not moved by hearing about all the fun that the seniors had because I could not stop thinking about the life changing experience I had the day before. I never knew how much people paid attention to me until I stopped being the center of attention. My experience forced me into a state of depression. I did not feel like the most popular guy in school who played 5 sports, President of the National Honors Society and a robotics team player with a 3.8 GPA. I felt like a failure who put on a facade for everybody and I was tired of feeling that way.

My oldest two brothers had moved into their own places and Deon was in college, so all the pressure was on me to make something happen in order for my mom and I to get out of this impoverished living. Ironically with a 3.8 GPA, I had no intentions on going to college. I had planned to get back in the streets and hustle just like my brothers did; after that wake-up call I decided I should probably go another route because I did not want to hurt my superman anymore. So, I decided to apply to one college and give it a try. Since I have experienced Michigan State University, I figured I would play it safe and apply. Funny thing is that I applied intentionally 3 weeks after the deadline so that I could get rejected. If I did not get accepted, then I would have a valid excuse as to why I should hustle again.

It was the beginning of March and I still had not heard from Michigan State University, so I began preparing for the streets. On March 11th, 2008, I received a letter of acceptance from Michigan State University. I was not as

83

proud as my mother was because all I could think about was *"am I ready for this change?", Am I smart enough for college? What if I'm not accepted? What if I don't finish, will people laugh at me?"*. Two weeks later, a very special lady friend of mine named Ta'Joina got accepted to Michigan State University as well, which made me more excited knowing that I wouldn't be alone. As I previously mentioned, I had a way with ladies and she was one of my "really special" friends, if you know what I mean.

The final months of my senior year were a breeze. I won class flirt, which I was not too surprised about, and I also won most likely to succeed and was confused as to why people believed in me so much. A couple weeks before graduation would be the prom, which I was excited for, one reason being that it was my first time getting a suit and another being that I was running for prom king against some other popular kids. I decided to take Kyra, seeing that she was the closet girl to me even after she knew I cheated on her.

The day of prom had lots of memorable moments. I wore an all cream suit with brown accessories to match Kyra's brown dress that fitted her body so well. Braids were freshly done the night before by an old special friend who was angry at how I handled our relationship, so my head still felt tight! I was able to purchase a limo with my cousin Antoine who had two dates. As we were outside taking pictures with our families I realized that my father was not there. I called him and asked him, "Hey Dad, we're taking pictures, where are you?".

"I'm 5 minutes away" he responded.

"Okay see you soon" I said and ended the call.

My father saying, "I'll be there in 5 minutes", quotes meant that he was not coming but I thought because of prom that he was serious. Unfortunately, he never came.

Once we arrived at prom Kyra decided to surprise me with a special treat inside of the limo before going into the building. So, when I entered the building I was already feeling like a king. It was great to see everybody in suits and women in dresses and not the black pants and white shirt uniforms that we were forced to wear. It was that time of the night when the prom king was announced. All of the candidates were next to the stage and I was in the back grabbing more punch. "And the winner is... Keyon Clinton", the announcer said. It felt like I'd won a Grammy seeing everybody turn around clapping and praising me. I was on a natural high for the entire night after winning.

On graduation day, I was informed that I was the salutatorian of the school with the second highest GPA of the school with a 3.84 GPA. Prior to walking on stage Mr. Wojekowski, my physics teacher, stopped me and apologized. He said "I am sorry I told you that you were never going to be anything in life. You are a bright kid and I just want you to believe in yourself because you have what it takes to go far in life". "Thank you, sir, I will not let you down", was my response. Walking across that stage was one of the greatest feelings in my life because the entire time I was looking at my mother's "Kool-Aid" smile and the tears falling profusely down her face. Thankfully, that was not the only time that I had seen my mother with that expression on her face. I never thought that due to a phone call I would instantly change my ways in some capacity, but I sure did.

CHAPTER 7: A CONVERSATION WITH MY FATHER

Before I started my new journey at Michigan State University, I did not want to take any baggage with me. I knew I needed to talk to my father because I had so much resentment toward him growing up. I prayed to God and asked him to give me the strength to listen to my father's story so that I could have some type of a relationship with him. The Bible says, in Exodus 20:12, "Honor your father and mother. Then you will live a long, full life in the land the LORD your God is giving you".

My mother and father split when I was 4 years old. Leon Tyner, my father, worked at Brother's Industries as a top hollow driver. He was making great money at the time. He was one of the best in the company, so they promoted him to a supervisor. He went into the company simply because the money was great, but after he became a specialist the job started requiring more and more of his time. The company owner, Richard Sykes, was my father's close friend from high school. Richard loved us so much that he allowed my father to bring us in on Saturdays and Sundays to learn about the process. This was a family owned company, so they promoted educating family first to run the business.

My father and mother were so in love at one time. My father was the bread winner making $1,100 a week. He was a church-going, noble, hardworking man. He used to take us to the drive-in every weekend where my parents would get Young's BBQ and buy us McDonald's. Going through the drive-in I remember my father telling us to duck down so that they did not see us. My father was the most organized man I knew. He even made sure we organized our toys in the closet. When Christmas came around, although we did not have a Christmas tree, we had so many toys that you could barely walk in the front room. Sixteen years of love is what my parents shared before the split.

Back in high school my father played for a great football team at Northeastern High School from 1978-1982. 1982 was the same year that the school was shutdown officially. My father was ranked as the number two football player in the world. He was the star running back, played guard and nose tackle. One fact that I loved the most about him was that he was a math whiz. The way he knew numbers was impeccable. His best friend was Hall of Famer, Isiah Thomas, who played for the Detroit Pistons. They were inseparable. I do not remember meeting him, but my mother would show us pictures that we took with him growing up.

My father had a full ride scholarship to Michigan State University, but he decided to turn it down because his grandmother was sick, and he wanted to take care of his children. My great grandfather had already passed, and my father was always a family man.

My great grandmother, Lucill Garris, died when he was 6 months old. She was in a relationship with BB King. Once my father was born, Lucil, had been away from the spotlight for a while. When she went back to the bar to see BB King, a woman in his entourage made it clear she did not like the connection between the two. A huge bar fight broke out leading to someone poisoning my grandmother at the bar and she passed away. BB King named his guitar Lucill in memory of my grandmother.

Once my father and his siblings reached adulthood, my great grandmother passed away. My father was a very dominant man. When he spoke, we would listen to him. A few things that he taught us were never to smoke cigarettes, to live with integrity and never stop believing in God because one day we will have to walk our own path.

When my father and mother split, things were different. I could not believe I would ever see the day. The more I watched my mother struggle the more I hated my father. *"How could you leave us in this position?"*, I thought. They decided to co-parent and honestly, I was not a fan of it. My mother got a new boyfriend and my father had a girlfriend. Meeting his new girlfriend was so awkward at first because we did not trust her at all. My father had to teach us at a young age how to catch 4 buses to school. I was so terrified catching the bus with my brothers at the age of 5.

One day, my mother got fed up with the way my father had been treating her and she decided to drop us off with him and his girlfriend. After that day, I did not see my mother for 5 years. We were too young to understand what was going on and we thought our mother was dead. My father was in a position where he was watching all four of us and taking care of his girlfriend's three children. He was at a bar drinking one day and he looked up and happened to see my mom with her new boyfriend. My father was talking to her new man George and asked my mother to come check on her kids.

My father was an honest man who was faced with a lot of challenges in life. He had to make the best out of his situation. We lived with him and a few of his lady friends but we made ends meet. I was hurt, confused, sad and lonely during this process. Then, one day, I remember seeing a car pull up at a BBQ we were at. I saw my mom hopping out the car and I ran as fast as I could into jump in her arms. I was too young to understand why she was gone, but in that moment, I did not care. I was just excited to see her alive.

After my mom was back in our lives, as a teenager I felt some type of way about her leaving. It caused me to look at her differently, so we began falling out. As much as I loved her, I just could not understand how she could leave us. After listening to my father, I had to ask him, "So why did you leave us, Pops?".

"I didn't leave y'all, your mom left me", he responded. "I only wanted the best for y'all. That's why I did everything I could from a distance without recognition from my kids", he said. I had grown up hating my father because I thought he decided to leave my mom for another woman.

"I needed you to teach me how to be a man. I made a lot of mistakes because of your absence", I said.

"I'm sorry, Son. I never planned to be away from my kids, I had to respect your mothers' wishes", he responded.

I had to realize that some of the things my father was doing he did not want us to witness or experience the effect of his actions. In that moment, I gained a newfound respect for my father. I did not know the full story, but after getting clarity, I lost the resentment. All I could do was focus on building a better relationship with him because he was an alcoholic and I did not want anything to happen to him. He always spoke highly of my mother, which I respected him for the most. As long as I have lived, I have never heard him talk down on my mother.

Growing up I was so mad at both of my parents for how they treated us despite the good things they did for us. Some of my childhood is a blur because I have been through so much. So, I hated my father for a lot of things that he did not do, but after this conversation I realized that he had sacrificed a lot for us. I knew I had to have this conversation and I was so thankful that I did because it lifted so much weight off of my shoulders. I was a little more prepared to go to college now but not quite all the way. It was time to enter a new chapter of my life.

CHAPTER 8: A COLLEGE KID WITH HOOD HABITS

After talking to my dad, I felt a load of resentment and stress lifted off me. I just felt I was headed to Michigan State University without any baggage, but boy was I wrong. It was the morning of August 15, 2008 and although everybody was happy for me to be headed to college, I was not as enthused.

"Good morning! It's your big day, I made you breakfast", my mother said.

I'm thinking to myself, *"Why is everybody happy for me? What if I fail?"*.

We'd packed the things in the car the night before so that my mother and I could get an early start on the road. Today was already peculiar because everybody was super happy, and I was not sure if they were genuinely happy for me or just happy to say they knew somebody who attended college. My cousins kept informing me over the summer that they could not wait to visit so that they could talk to the girls. My uncle would ask about my refund check so that I could loan him some money that he would never pay back even though he promised to. My female cousins were only interested in the athletes.

Although I was looking forward to the freedom of being away from my mother's house rules, I did not want to move away too far, so moving 1 hour and 30 minutes to East Lansing was not a bad choice.

"I am just so proud of you, Son. I always knew you would grow up and be a smart young man", my mother said to me. "Thanks Mom", I uttered softly.

"What's wrong, Keyon? All morning you've been dragging like today isn't special. What's bothering you?", my mother asked. I took a deep breath and responded, "I just don't get why everyone is so happy. I don't know anything about college. What if I fail? Antonio and Leon both went to college and dropped out. Deon is in college but he's struggling too. It just doesn't seem like we were made to go to college". "Everybody's path is different, Keyon. I know you look up to your brothers, but just because they didn't finish doesn't mean that you have to repeat the same thing. We are excited for you because we believe in you! You have the chance to do something that has never been done before and that makes me happy. All I ask is that you do your best and I will be thankful for whatever the outcome is", my mother replied. From that moment, I started to change my perspective and started to believe that I was smart and deserved to be in college.

Being that this was my very first-time leaving Detroit I was enjoying the "scenic route" heading to Michigan State University. Later I realized that my route was not scenic, I just had not been outside of Detroit, LOL. After feeling liberated for about an hour and fifteen minutes, that feeling changed when I saw the sign "Welcome to Michigan State University". I psyched myself into thinking I would fit in, but once we arrived on campus and I saw all of the people, instantly I knew that this was a bad decision. Everyone seemed happy and peaceful and here I was coming from this broken background. I knew I did not stand a chance.

The dorm I lived in was called "Akers Hall" and I was going in blind with 3 roommates. Once we got registered and approved to unload, I started unpacking my things into a bin.

"Hello and welcome to MSU", some random person said to me. In my head I was thinking, *"Why is this stranger talking to me and why is she so happy?"*. Where I was from you had to be skeptical of any suspicious activity.

"What's up?", I responded.

"My name is Lisa and I am here to assist you with your move in. Do you need any help getting to your room?" she asked.

"No thank you, I believe I know where it is", I said.

"Perfect! Just let me know if you need anything", Lisa responded and walked away. I looked around and saw so many different races that I had never seen before. That was my first culture shock.

"Keyon! Let's go see your room", my mother said, snapping me out of shock. As I opened the door to my room in Akers Hall, thankfully I was the first one to arrive. Having the option to choose which side I wanted to live on gave me a sense of empowerment. I was "claiming my turf". After we unpacked the last load, my mom and I sat in my room and talked. "Are you ready, Son?", my mom asked.

"For what?", I replied.

"To be great! I know this may be different and challenging, but I believe in you. You have your family's support, whenever you need us just call. I cannot tell you how proud of you I am. I love you so much", my mother said. Her words calmed my spirit and gave me a sense of hope.

"Thank you, Ma, I appreciate that. I am going to need your support because I cannot do it alone. I am scared to be honest, but we are survivors, so I will not come back without a degree. I love you too", I replied.

As we were walking to her car, I could feel the tears starting to run down my face. Seeing my mother leave made me feel alone in a different world with no guidance. "Don't cry; I will come visit you often. It will be okay", my mother said. Little did I know that her "visit you often" would only come 7 years later.

After sitting in my room and unpacking for an hour I heard knocks on the door. I figured it was one of my roommates, but it was the residential assistant. "Hey, I am Victoria and I am your residential assistant for this floor. My office is down the hall and if you need any help with anything just come down, I have an open-door policy", she said.

"Thank you, I sure will", I responded.

"Are your roommates here?" Victoria asked.

"No, not yet", I replied.

"Well, come with me, I can introduce you to some people", Victoria insisted.

As we were walking to the middle of the floor, we approached this six-foot light-skinned guy on a bike. "Keyon, this is Darius", Victoria said. She got a call and had to go assist other people, so I was in this area with a stranger.

"What's good? I'm Keyon", I said.

"What's the deal? I'm Darius", he responded.

"That's a nice bike, did you bring it from home?" I asked.

"Oh this, naw I just seen it lying around so I took it", Darius responded. In that moment, as crazy as this may sound, I knew we would be friends, LOL.

"I need to find me a bike lying around too", I responded.

As we continued to get to know each other a little more he informed me of a party going on later and at that time I could use some excitement, so I told him I would go.

As I walked back to my room, I noticed that my door was open. My hood defense mode came out. I creeped up to my door to see if I would catch anybody stealing anything only to find one of my roommates unpacking their things. I was thinking to myself *"Another black dude, great!"*. "What's good, bro? I'm Keyon", I said.

"Hey bro, I'm Terrian, nice to meet you", he responded.

I started to help him unload his belongings and I asked him, "Where are you from?".

"Detroit. The west side", he responded. As much as I disliked the west side of Detroit, I decided to let him get a pass because we were at school and plus he was my roommate.

After he was settled into the room I told him about the Darius guy and the party, which he was okay with going to.

We met in our room around 9 p.m. to pregame. As we began walking up the main street Grand River, looking like 3 lost freshmen, we ran into a group of freshmen girls who were looking for the same party. We connected and started walking together. Moments later, cars started driving past us blowing their horns. At this point I was very intoxicated and confused. "Why are they blowing their horns?" one of the girls asked.

Then, as a car was riding by blowing its horn, a guy was hanging out the passenger window saying, "Freshmen go home". I was introduced to one of the traditions that the upperclassmen had here at MSU. Around midnight, we finally found the party. Between the loud music, beautiful girls, and alcohol, I was in paradise. Darius walked up to me and said, "You ready to have the wildest first night of college?".

"I was made for this", I responded.

We walked into the house and my eyes lit up. Women grinding on the men, kissing taking place and freedom to do whatever we wanted to do. I was never a big drinker entering college, but for some reason that thought did not cross my mind when I was asked if I wanted something to drink. For the very first time I was introduced to beer pong. Beer was never my forte, but with so much freedom I did not care what I was drinking.

After getting intoxicated from the beer and alcohol, a girl walked up to me and said, "You're cute, want to dance?". In my mind, I was thinking, *Duh*, but I had to play it cool so that she did not think that I was freshman. "Of course", I replied. We walked off to find a space on the wall, and I will never forget the song to my very first dance in college, "Let Me Lick You Up and Down" by Keith Sweat.

In that moment, I experienced the difference between high school and college women. The slow gyration and seductive movements were the best feeling ever. She turned around and faced me then began to grind closely on my leg. With my hands on her booty I was thinking to myself *"I can get used to this. Tonight, may be a lucky night for me if I play my cards right"*.

Just when I had built up the courage to ask her for her phone number, I heard police sirens and saw flashing lights; the police were telling everybody to go home. The girl I danced with left to go find her girls and I never saw her again. Although I did not get her number, I did enjoy the party. Darius and I linked up outside and I told him about the girl. He was excited and told me about a girl he danced with as well. Once we got back to our rooms, I reflected on my day and felt a lot better than I had when my mother had left.

During the first week of school, Michigan State University had a "Welcome Back" week where they put on different programs and networking events for the freshmen to get acclimated with campus and to welcome back the upperclassmen to a new year. Darius and I attended the events to meet new people, learn about different organizations and just socialize. I have never seen so many people in one space in my life. After conversing and learning about organizations, I started to feel confident about being a Spartan. The first days of my courses were filled with going over the syllabi and expectations from the professors.

On Thursday August 14, 2008, I vividly remember walking to my dorm from class. As I was heading home on this sunny day I watched an all-yellow Lamborghini cruising on Shaw Street. Coming from Detroit, Michigan, the only time I would see a Lamborghini was in my dreams. Instantly I started to freak out to the point where I tapped a random guy and asked him, "Did you just see that?".

He responded with excitement "Bro, what? That's my dream car!" In that moment, I had no idea that I was meeting my best friend to this day. After spending 5 minutes appreciating that moment of greatness we came back to normal. "I'm Keyon bro" I said to him.

"I'm Deon'ta but you can call me Tae" he responded.

"Where you headed?" I asked.

"Akers Hall", he said. "You?".

"That's where I live. You stay there too?" I asked.

"No, my friend lives there on the third floor", he responded.

After that, I told him that I lived on the third floor as well, and we got to know more about each other on that walk. I came to find out the girl he was going to visit was roommates with a lady I had just recently met. This interaction could not have been more divine. Instead of going to my room, I decided to go with Tae to the girls' room down the hall. After spending an hour or so talking and laughing, Tae and I went to my room where I introduced him to my roommate. I found out that he was from the west side of Detroit, and although I was not a fan of west siders, I gave him a pass because he seemed to be a cool guy.

A few weeks later Darius, Tae and I were sitting in the lobby of Akers Hall observing the scenery when we met a guy by the name of Trammel Brown, a down-to-earth guy from the east side of Detroit so we instantly became friends.

Ten years later, those gentlemen are still my closest friends to this day.

Freshman year was full of excitement for me. Lots of drinking, smoking, women and freedom. I was living in the fast lane. Our popularity grew rapidly because of the activities we would engage in. We stayed on the in-crowd of everything, so our names stayed relevant as the new kids on campus. Even through all of the fast living after my freshman year I was able to maintain a 3.6 GPA overall on the year. My mother was super happy to hear that her baby boy was doing great in college. I remember going home to work at Family Dollar for the summer and I hated it. Getting a taste of college let me know that, as much as I loved my city, I was not missing anything but the same people doing the same things every day. I was excited about going back to school because of the ice breakers and reuniting with my friends.

A reality check set in real fast when we got back to school and some of the people we met were not able to come back because of their poor grades. Academic probation was death to many college students at that time. As a sophomore in college the nervousness was completely gone. I was not a new student and people knew who I was.

I figured this year would be a breeze. As the cycle of living the fast lane continued, my friends and I started to hit some road blocks. From getting into arguments and fights with guys who did not like us to women issues and excessive drug use, things started to get bad for me. I realized that I had started drinking to cope with my family issues and financial struggles. I began feeling like I was living in Detroit again.

My junior year I moved off campus because I needed some more freedom. Deon'ta, Mel, Terrian and I decided to get an apartment together. I got accepted into the college of engineering, so I figured that maybe I should start taking school more seriously. I had my doubts and insecurities about if I could really be an electrical engineer. The first two years of prerequisite courses were easy, but actual engineering courses challenged me in ways that I struggled with. None of the students wanted to work with me because I was not the typical engineer. The culture shock that I was experiencing was mind-blowing. I noticed that most engineers were anti-social with a weird vibe. I was the student who did not know much so I always asked others for their help with homework or looked over their shoulders on exam day.

My level of frustration grew because not only was I struggling with my courses, this was my third year and I still had not landed an internship or co-op. None of the mock interview trainings and tips from career services were any help for me in landing a job for the summer. I met a friend who introduced me to a pill called Adderall. Adderall to engineering students was like giving a 5-course meal to a homeless person who haven't eaten in weeks. Although I never tried it, the 48205 spirit in me knew I could sell it. Within the first 3 month of selling Adderall, I was making so much money I realized that I did not need an on-campus job. Only reason I kept my job because it was a part of my work study tuition and I knew I could not afford to lose any financial aid. It got so bad that students will figure out my class schedule and be waiting on me to get out of class to get some Adderall. Word got out and I started to get this feeling that something bad was going to happen soon. One day I walked into the Diversity Programs Office where all the students meet and do homework and the mood was peculiar.

"You heard what happened to your boy?", Matt said.

"Naw, what happened?', I asked.

"He got caught selling Adderall to students and now he's getting kicked out of school", he responded.

I left campus sick to my stomach hoping that he wouldn't snitch on me. I prayed to God and told him that I was tired of putting myself in the same messed up predicaments. I was sitting in my bedroom thinking to myself that it was time for a change. I was tired of feeling like I was throwing away a good opportunity because of my poor choices. It was time to change my habits and surround myself with people who could elevate my life. I had a thought of joining a fraternity my sophomore year, but I never acted on it.

As I went through the list of fraternities, I knew I did not want to bark like a dog, I was not a pretty boy, and being that I had two older brothers who were Sigmas, I thought the Sigmas at Michigan State were really weird individuals so that turned me off about them and the Iotas were trying too hard to be tough for me. It was a no brainer that Alpha Phi Alpha Fraternity Incorporated was the best choice of men who would groom me into the man I wanted to become. So, I started doing my research on the fraternity's existence and the amount of history and impact literally amazed me. Alpha men were heavily involved in almost every monumental event in the black community. The Alphas on Michigan State's campus were the only group educating the people on current events, social issues and seemed to genuinely care about the community. So, my decision was made.

The next day, I walked up to my friend Justin who was an Alpha and I still did not know what to expect when trying to join a fraternity, so I asked him "what's good, bro?".

"What's good, G?", he responded.

"I'm trying to join this Alpha shit, bro", I said to him.

He busted out laughing. "Key, you ain't ready for this, G, stop playing", he responded.

"I'm dead serious, bro, it's time for a change", I said.

"Come to our informational and then we can go from there", Justin said.

So, I thought it would be smart to reach out to other Alphas who were on the yard to show my interest. One of the Alphas I did not care much for because of our previous interactions. His name was Paris Wilson who had major influence on the yard, so I knew I needed to talk to him soon. I reached out to set up a meeting and when he agreed, I was shocked. I walked in his room and I could feel the tension from his body language. "So, what's up?", Paris said.

"I wanted to talk to you about becoming a member of your fraternity", I said.

He busted out laughing at me and said, "Why?".

I was a little offended, but I knew I had to keep my composure so that I did not mess up my chances. "Because I believe in the mission and aims of the fraternity. I love the brotherhood and would like to surround myself with men who will help me go to the next level", I responded.

This drew another sarcastic laugh from Paris. "Honestly Keyon, you're too ghetto for my fraternity. We don't need people like you", he responded. At that moment I knew his personal feelings were involved. He was still bitter because a female that he used to talk to stopped talking to him once I met her. Although I wanted to say something ignorant, I refrained and said, "I am changing every day and I believe this would be the perfect place to change my life. Thanks for the conversation and have a good day".

After I left his room I started thinking to myself, *Am I too ghetto to be a part of a prestigious group?* Then I realized that, in order to be great, I had to surround myself with great men, so nothing was going to stop me from becoming a member. I attended the informational and, surprisingly, I saw a few guys I knew. The Alphas talked about the origin and history of the fraternity, what they did as a chapter on Michigan State's campus and what it took to become an Alpha man. I connected with some of the other interests so that we could become friends prior to our journey if we were selected.

Two weeks later, I received a call notifying me that I had been selected to embark upon the journey of becoming an Alpha man. Tears of joy fell down my face because I felt like this was God giving me another chance to get my life together. Not only had I been selected by the Alphas to move forward in the process, I was also selected by the other interests to be the president of our line. Now this was great news until I realized that I had to do the majority of the speaking and lord knows I hated speaking in front of people.

During my process, everything you think could have gone wrong did! My mother got sick; my car broke down; all of my accounts were in the negative; my classes got dropped randomly; I got an eviction notice, was placed on probation at work for being late and I had a family member die. My life was filled with anxiety, stress, depression and pain but I kept pushing through. This is how I received the nickname Bulletproof.

I remember talking to Paris about all of the things that I was going through in hopes that he would provide me with some words of encouragement. His response was, "Life goes on, Keyon". In that moment I felt like that was the most insensitive thing someone could ever say to a person in pain. The thoughts of hurting him badly were flowing all through my brain because I felt disrespected, but I knew I could not do anything to ruin my chances. After a few weeks I started to understand the meaning behind his tough love. In life there are things that are beyond our control so there is no point in giving too much energy to them. If I would have quit during my process, I still would have had the same issues going on. Thankfully, I was going through this process with 10 men who were right next to me the entire time. Denzel Wright, Henry Ward, Kenneth Jackson, Brannon Bass, Veotis Thompson, Tyler Hendon, Tyler Clifford, Dedrick Cotton II, Marvin Harbour and Charles Colson were the 10 men I started and finished the process with. We are known as T.H.E.G.I.F.T.

After the process it was time for the probate so that we could be introduced to the campus. Not only was this a big day for me because I was about to reveal myself to the world as an Alpha man, this day was also important to me because I had to cut my braids off after having them for 21 years of my life. I was becoming a new man and to watch them cut my hair off in front of my mom was hard to experience. As we locked up and marched to the location, I could hear the screams from the crowd growing louder and louder. When my dean removed the mask from my Ace and

I saw the reaction of the crowd, my heart started pounding because I knew I was next.

"From the east side of Detroit, majoring in electrical engineering, in Alpha Land we know him as ISSA, but you know him as Keyon Clinton", my dean said and removed my mask. I have never heard that many people scream for me till this day. So much adrenaline was rushing through my body. It was truly an outer body experience for me. After we all were released and did our steps we fellowshipped with our family and friends. It felt so good to be completely done and free.

The next day, I walked into class and the professor said, "Excuse me, sir, are you lost?". I just busted out laughing because she could not tell who I was without the hair. "It's me, Keyon. I just cut my hair off on Monday", I said. She was in shock but then gave me a compliment although I knew it was fake. I looked crazy with a bald head and no facial hair, but I appreciated her not embarrassing me in front of the class.

Things began heading in the right direction for my life. A week later, I was called by Chrysler regarding an internship opportunity at their headquarters. My heart was filled with joy. After I got my first internship, I secured 3 more and a co-op throughout my collegiate career. My sixth year at Michigan State, my new brand was well established. The old wild and reckless Keyon was gone. I held the president, vice president, and chaplain positions within the fraternity and I became a voice for the community. I began asking myself, *"What can I leave behind so that my legacy will live on forever? How can I create an environment where people from all races, ethnic groups and backgrounds can come together and push each other to succeed in different facets of life?"*. So, I prayed and asked God to reveal to me my purpose and he put the word "family" on my heart. Everybody who knew me; knew that I showed love for my family and that I was a selfless person who loved people. As I began to realize that I was no longer living for myself, God gave me the clarity. F.A.M.I.L.Y. "Forget About Me, I Love You!".

I jumped on my bed screaming like I'd found a million dollars. I knew this was it. I put the mission, vision, objectives and logo together and marinated on it for another month. When I felt that it was time to present it, I released it to Michigan State University. The amount of support and gratitude I received was-mind blowing. Typically, programs would have an attendance of 30-40 people, but my program's average was around 70 plus. The purpose of my organization was in the name. Sacrificing self-gratification for the success of others is what we are all about. I knew it was time for a team, so I created a calling for an executive board. The amount of applications and interest were overwhelming, but I knew I was on to something with this movement. In the 3 months of existence we obtained 40 members, worked with the Magic Johnson Foundation, made the state news twice for our work in the community and hosted over 8 programs. The entire campus was talking about F.A.M.I.L.Y. As happy as I was, I started to realize that I would graduate the next year and the question of who would run the organization came to mind. I sat down with my vice president to express my feelings and vision moving forward after I left. I expressed to him that this was my purpose and that I needed for him to take care of the organization after me. He assured that he would watch me closely and learn so that he could be better than I was. With that reassurance, I knew the organization would be in good hands.

The summer before my seventh and last year, I worked an internship at Dow Chemical in Midland, Michigan. I was not a fan of the company, but they paid great money so that was enough for me to accept the position. There was literally nothing to do for fun in Midland, so I went back to campus every weekend.

One weekend, my bruhs were throwing a house gathering and I was excited to party with them. The entire campus knew that whenever T.H.E.G.I.F.T. threw a party you needed to be there. The apartment was so packed that people could barely move so people started migrating outside to the parking lot. After about two hours of fun the police pulled up to shut down the party. I had taken some shots and was feeling buzzed, but I knew I had to get back so that I could work in the morning. My line brother, Tyler Hendon, came up to me and said, "Aye Key, you think you should leave this late? I think you should just wait till the morning, bro".

"Naw, I'm good, bro, it's only 45 minutes away, plus I don't want to wake up extra early to drive", I responded.

"Okay please make sure you let me know when you made it, bro, please", Tyler said.

I was on the road struggling to see because my headlights were dying out and it was dark on the freeway. After about 20 minutes into the drive I was thinking to myself, *only 25 more minutes to go.* Out of nowhere a buck ran into my lane and looked me dead in the face. Before I could turn the wheel, it was too late. I hit the buck and the antlers cracked my entire windshield as I spun out into a ditch. My heart was pounding profusely. I thought my leg was broken because of the pain and there was literally no one around. The first person I called was my line brother, Tyler. "Bro, please help, Ty, I got in an accident on the freeway. Please, I'm hurting", I screamed.

Tyler's panic button kicked in as he asked me where I was.

"I don't know, on the freeway. It's dark, hurry", I said.

"Okay we're on the way", Tyler said.

Then, I called my brother Deon because I knew that, even though he was in Detroit, he would always be there for me. Plus, I felt like I was dying so I needed to talk to someone in my family and send my love. "Dee, bro, I got in an accident, I'm hurting, help me, Bro", I said.

He instantly woke up and started asking where I was.

"What's hurting?"

"Everything hurt. I don't know where I am, Bro, call Tyler", I said. I gave him Tyler's number and hung up.

I laid back in the chair and said, "God, please don't let me die tonight". Out of nowhere I heard a voice saying, "Do you need some help?". To this day I could not tell you who it was, but I know it was the voice of a woman.

"Yes please, I'm hurting", I responded.

That was the last thing I remember before passing out. I woke up in the back of an ambulance, confused at first. I saw my line brothers there, which made me feel good. Thankfully, nothing was broken or heavily damaged. I suffered some deep bruises on my leg and contusions in my hands and arm. Lying in the hospital bed all I could think about was that life is precious and at any moment it can be taken away from you. My brother made it to the hospital and seeing him made everything feel better. He is my rock and has never missed a special or tragic moment in my life.

Unfortunately, that was the highlight of my summer, but thankfully I was able to recover fully and buy a new car.

Walking into my last year at Michigan State University, I was so proud of getting there. At this point I had been to thirteen graduations and on the fourteenth one, I would be walking across the stage. With Alpha, F.A.M.I.L.Y. and school going well, I knew this year would be a breeze. I had senioritis for the past three years at this point and was ready to go. Lots of partying and celebration took place my last year.

The biggest thing on my mind, though, was securing a full-time job. Six months prior to graduating, I got a call from Marathon to come out to their headquarters for my final interview. I was excited to go crush the interview and receive a full-time position. I loaded up the rental to drive to Findlay, Ohio for my interview and I remember telling Tae to watch my car. I'd purchased a 2010 Dodge Charger, so I thought I was moving up in the world. About an hour and a half into the ride I got a call from Tae informing me that a man was at the house to repossess my car.

"Bro, stop playing with me", I said.

"Key, I'm dead serious. He said he will let me get anything out of it before he takes it", Tae responded.

I could not believe this. I knew I was late on a couple payments, but I did not think they would take the car. I tried to remain positive because I was heading to a situation that could change my life forever. *"I'm tired of living in the struggle,"*, I said to myself. I went into the interview confident and I crushed it like I always do. Now I just had to wait on the call to see if I got the job or not.

I got back home and went to the dealership to see if there was anything that I could do to get my car back. The woman who worked there informed me that I could not because of late payments. Back to the bus and asking people for rides until I got a new car. I remember lying to people, telling them I got into an accident, because I was embarrassed to tell the truth about what happened. I literally went to every dealership in Lansing and was denied by all of them due to my bad credit.

I figured that I'd get a job with a signing bonus and then just get a new car before I started a new job. I got a job with ArcelorMittal and they gave me a ten-thousand-dollar relocation fund, which gave me the financial capital to make a down payment on a nice car.

Graduation day was here, and it was time to do something that was so rare in my family. It was time to walk across a college stage for a degree. My entire family came up to experience that moment with me. As I walked across the stage, I created a note that read, "Momma, I will retire you soon!".

After I showed that note on the big screen I heard the entire audience go, "Awww", then I saw the biggest smile on my mother's face. It was one of the greatest moments of my life because I made everybody proud. This college kid with hood habits still made it through without quitting.

CHAPTER 9: LIVING IN F.E.A.R.

There is a plethora of reasons why people may not succeed in life, but I believe that the determining factor in why most people have yet to reach the success that they have envisioned, is because of the F.E.A.R. factor. Everybody wants to be successful, but people are afraid of the lifestyle changes they must make and the sacrifices that are needed to reach optimal success. That is because people look at fear from the wrong level of perspective. The Bible says in Proverbs 1:7, "Fear of the Lord is the foundation of knowledge, but fools will despise wisdom and instruction".

So, I asked God, "Why do you want me to be afraid of you?'. If I am afraid of you, I will not be as willing to exalt your name, nor will I be as receptive to building a relationship with you".

In the Old Testament, the meaning of fear is awe, reverence and obedience to the Lord not to be afraid of him. So F.E.A.R. has two meanings: initially, its Forget Everything And Run; but when you change your level of perspective it then becomes Face Everything And Rise. You ever wonder why people jump off buildings, play with lions and bears, or do some of the most outlandish things in the world? It is not because they are crazy or that they are trying to become famous for their stunts, it is because they have literally removed the presence of fear from their lives. Most people have this big fear of failure. One of my favorite quotes is from Thomas Edison "I have not failed. I've just found 10,000 ways that won't work". There is no such thing as failure. I believe that when things do not work out for you that is just God telling you not right now. Also, everything that happens in life is either a lesson or a blessing so when things do not go as planned hopefully you have learned from your experience and you are better prepared for next time.

I remember being a child and watching actors and television hosts while thinking to myself, *I could never be on television.* I was so afraid of success due to my current circumstances that I could not even think of or envision myself doing great things. When you walk around living in fear, you directly and indirectly miss out on so many opportunities in life. It was not until I started believing in me that I made a name for myself around Detroit and other states because of my confidence and influence. Before I knew it, I was featured on WDIV Channel 4 local news station for a Fitness Friday segment. I was also featured on a few other local television networks in Detroit as well. What I have learned is that fear is a mental thing. Once you train and condition your mind that all things are possible, then fear becomes a non-factor. Most people never face their fears because they do not know where to start.

I believe the starting point is awareness. Before you can begin overcoming fear, you must be aware that your fears are causing havoc in your life. It is easy to get so attached to your thoughts and feelings that you think they are all that exists, which could not be further from the truth. You are not your fears. You are the awareness that experiences them. Then you must identify your fears. Get specific about what exactly you're afraid of. Look at the pictures you have in your head about the situation. What is happening in them? What are you really scared of? Become an observer of your inner space. Once you identify with your fears you must convert your feelings into gratitude. Whenever you feel fear, switch it over to what you are grateful for instead. If you're afraid of public speaking, be grateful for the opportunity to communicate with so many people and that they are there to genuinely listen to what you have to say. Now you are replacing the negatives with the positives, which will produce a better outcome.

Always remember that it is the little things that can produce big results when overcoming your fears. Another habit to overcome fears is journaling. Getting your fears down on paper is important because trying to think them through does not always work. You can get caught in endless loops of negativity that only lead you to more stress and fear, making your life miserable.

One of the most effective ways to overcome fear is to simply talk it out. Ask yourself how often do we hold the negative in because we are afraid of how others might react or because of some other reason? Talking helps, but don't throw a pity party for yourself. The goal is to address the fear and find a solution to rectify it, not have everybody feeling empathy for you.

Then, after you speak with your confidant, the last thing that will be beneficial in overcoming your fears is putting things into the right perspective. Learning to deal with fear is all about putting your negative thoughts into perspective. We tend to focus too much on the negative. By looking at all the options, you often realize that you're making a big deal out of nothing. There are so many things that can happen that are impossible for you to predict. We are not psychics, we are human beings. Expect the worst because it may happen but expect the best because it will happen.

Once I gained the confidence that I could do whatever I put my mind to I became an Execution Coach. My expertise is simply executing! I specialize in helping others execute in certain areas of their lives to build confidence and provide clarity on their true purpose in life. I do this by pushing them to a level of uncomfortability. What I have learned in my 27 years of living is that people hate to be pushed and they hate to be uncomfortable. They fail to realize that it is in their level of uncomfortability that true growth is formed.

There are 4 areas of life that I like to focus on to help you develop drive. The first is confidence. Confidence is a stain that nobody can wipe off. I believe that confidence is the source of everything else in your life because if you are confident in who you are and confident in who your God is then you understand that you have nothing to worry about. Second is intentionality. Be intentional with the things you say because you cannot take your words back. Be intentional in the things you do because it sucks to have to apologize for treating others wrong. Most importantly, be intentional with the people you have in your life because your confidants can be the reason for your success or the reason for your destruction.

Next is purpose. There is a big difference between living an active life and living a purposeful life. Ask God to reveal his purpose for your life and watch how things change drastically. Never live life on a treadmill. That is where you are doing a lot of things whether it is starting businesses or getting degrees and certifications just to build up your accomplishments. The reality is that no matter how much movement that is taking place in your life there is no forward progress just like being on a treadmill. You want to make sure that you are not just making moves but that you are making power moves.

Last is self-sufficiency. It is time for us to take ownership over our own lives. Only you can control your destiny, but you must protect your peace and preserve your energy. Always remember that, no matter how dark your past was, you have the ability to make your future as bright as you want it to be. Now that I am afraid of nothing, I walk around with a perspective of forward thinking and continuous progression in life. Fear is simply a thought that only you have the power to change. Are you ready to change it?

CHAPTER 10: 2017

On December 12th, 2016, around 9:30pm in the evening, I heard knocking on the front door. I was little startled because I was not expecting company at that time of the night. As I opened the door I saw a white man standing there with a cowboy hat, a white tee shirt, blue jeans and some cowboy boots. "How can I help you, sir?", I asked.

"Hello is the tenant of the house available?", he asked.

"I am the tenant, sir, just my mom and I live here", I responded. He proceeded to say, "Well my name is Jared and I wanted to inform you that the current landlord lost the deeds to the house".

"Okay you came here to tell me that, what does that have to do with us?" I responded.

"Due to her not paying the back taxes, I just became the new owner by purchasing this house in an auction", he said.

My face dropped hearing this devastating news from this stranger. "Well, sir, here are the receipts for the last year and a half of the rent being paid on time", I said to him. After going through every payment, I proceeded to say, "As you can see, I am a responsible tenant, is there a way that we can create a contract to stay in the house?".

"Well, I am sorry that this happened to you and I see that you are a responsible tenant, but I purchased this house so that I can move my mother in here. Unfortunately, I have to ask for you to be out of here within the next two weeks", he said.

My heart literally fell into my stomach. I could not believe what I'd just heard. It was mid-December, a blizzard outside and we had nowhere to go. My mother arrived home around 11:30 p.m. and my heart was pounding as I sat on the couch with my head down. As she walked in the door I spoke with a monotone. "Hey Ma".

"What's wrong with you?", she responded.

"Have a seat, Ma, I need to tell you something. So, a guy came here about two hours ago telling me that the landlord lost the deeds to the house because she wasn't paying back taxes".

"What!", she shouted.

"I know, Ma. What makes it even worse is that he wasn't willing to let us stay here. He said we have two weeks to move out", I informed her. I saw the tears starting to fall down her face. This was the same face of the woman I had seen being put out of homes multiple times throughout my childhood.

"Don't cry, Ma, we will get through this. Try to get you some rest, I'll make a few calls and see what I can do", I said.

Sleeping for me was out of the question because all I could think about was what were we going to do. I spent the entire night on the computer looking up houses for rent, apartments, storage units and laws on eviction until I eventually passed out. I woke up wishing that it was all a dream until reality set in.

I took the day off on December 13th, 2016 to call houses and apartments for appointments to visit; I drove around the city of Detroit looking for rent signs and contacting the companies. After the first week of calling and visiting places, I made no progress towards finding a place. Now the pressure was on. My mother, who worked 16 hours a day, had no time to assist in the house search and my brothers were living with their wives and children so they did not have room for an additional two more bodies. I got into contact with a storage unit because it seemed that we would not find a place to move into before we were evicted. On Christmas Day, while the world was spending time with their loved ones and singing jolly songs of Christmas, my mother and I were moving our things into a storage unit with nowhere to go. I have been evicted a lot of times in my life but this one hurt the most. At 26 years of age with a college degree and being a full-time electrical engineer, I could not believe that this was happening to me. I'm educated, I make good money and I am living a good positive life is what I was thinking to myself.

My mother came home from work the following day and informed me that her coworker would allow her to move in with her, but she was going to decline her offer.

"Why, Ma?", I asked.

"Because where will you go, Keyon?", she replied.

"I know I'm your youngest son, Ma, but I am a grown man, I'll figure it out. As long as you're safe I can live with that. I know people and have friends I can call and, besides, with my credit and job we will have a new place within a couple days", I responded.

My mom continued to plead her case as to why she did not want to leave me out, but I convinced her to go stay with her coworker and we would work things out soon. I remember praying to God and telling him on December 26th, 2017 that I was going to fully surrender to him. I was unsure as to why these events were taking place in my life, but I knew that I needed to have faith in order to get through it. After my prayer I felt relieved because I just knew everything was going to be alright.

I woke up in the morning and called my brother Deon who I know always has my back no matter what. I asked him if he and his wife would mind me coming over for a couple of weeks until I could find a place to live. Thankfully they had just moved into a place with a basement, so they had a little space for me to stay. I spent the entire day calling houses and scheduling house visits. I was able to book ten visitations, so I was in a pretty good mood. I took a walk around the block to clear my head from all of the negative thoughts and doubts that were in there. *I am moving from Detroit to Inkster so that's going to be a long drive to work,* was one thought that I was thinking to myself. *I have to wake up earlier, I have to prep my food and clothes the night before so that I am organized.* My life and how I was currently living was about to change drastically. I couldn't go in whenever I liked because this was not my house, I could not have company over because I had to respect my brother and his family. Plus, nobody wanted to drive all the way to Inkster to be in a basement, so I had to use a lot more gas getting to places.

The walk provided me an understanding of what I was moving into and made me realize that I needed to find my own space immediately because I did not like living under people's rules. After walking back to the empty house, I reminisced on all of my old memories that I had there. Once I felt a few tears running down my face I snapped out of it and told myself to man up and move forward in life. Easier said than done.

I drove to my first house appointment and I was excited. This 3-bedroom house looked beautiful on the internet, so I could not wait to see the inside. I walked inside the house and was greeted by the steward who was showing off the place. This was the first of many disappointments I would soon experience. The lovely carpet on the internet had so many stains in real life. The walls were painted 3 different colors. The kitchen was dirty, and the basement was not finished at all. "Why do the pictures on the internet look so different?" I asked the steward. "I know that sometimes they keep the older pictures up there to make the house look more appealing", she responded. I was thinking, *so they do not care about false advertisements, I see.*

After leaving, I headed to the Burger King up the street for some food. While I was in the drive-through ordering, a guy walked up to my car trying to sell me some DVDs. "I'm not interested", I informed him, but it seemed as if he did not want to take no for an answer. *Lord, I just want my food so that I can go home.* He then walked around to my window and began telling me about all of the bootleg movies. "Sir, I said no thank you!", I said loudly. Detroiters never take no for an answer the first time.

Once I left Burger King I went back to my house to call more houses to find somewhere to live. I scheduled 10 house visits in the next two days. *Out of ten places, one of them has to be a good quality house,* was the thought going through my head. I spent the rest of the day cleaning up the last few miscellaneous things around the house and disinfecting everything. My mom came home around 11:00 p.m. so I made sure she had dinner waiting for her.

This was our last night being in the house. I could sense the sadness on my mother's face as she was eating. "Everything is going to be alright, Ma", I said.

"I know, Son. I'm just tired of going through this in my life. I've been getting evicted since before you were born and I'm starting to lose hope", my mom said. Seeing my superman defeated I really did not know what to say or do.

"Ma, God gives his toughest battles to his hardest soldiers. I know things don't seem to be okay at this moment, but you can't lose faith. The fact that you've been through this so many times should show you that God is going to turn things around just like he did every other time", I responded.

"You're right. So where are you going to stay?", she asked.

"I'm going to live with Deon for a while, but I did schedule 10 house visits, so we'll have a house in no time", I responded.

These next two days that I planned were supposed to be full of excitement and joy choosing which house I wanted to move into, but instead it was a disaster. Every house was a disappointment. After getting settled in at my brother's house the first month it went better than I had expected. They understood my situation, so they did not have an issue with me staying. I was able to spend a lot of time with my nephew, which was the best part of my day. My mom worked at Citi Trends in Southfield, Michigan, and my gym was in the same plaza, so I made sure that I checked on her every day.

"Any luck on the house search?", she asked one day.

"Not at all. They all suck", I responded.

"Well, keep on looking, eventually something will come through", she said.

"I will. Love you, Ma. Talk to you tomorrow", I said as I was walking out the store. After the gym I went to my brother's house and got right on the computer to look up houses.

Two more months passed by and my level of frustration began to rise, but I had to keep my composure because I vowed to God that I would trust him. At this point

I had already been sleeping in my car because I had noticed that my stay at my brothers was becoming somewhat of an inconvenience to his family. Married couples cannot live freely with a guest in the house, so I had to respect and understand that.

March 9th, 2017 I was leaving a Walmart and I saw these flashing lights behind me. "Fuck! It's the police", I said out loud. At the time there was a storm taking place, so I was even more irritated and on top of that I was leaving in the morning to head to Miami for a vacation that was overdue.

"Hey officer did I do something wrong?", I asked.

"License and registration please", he responded.

"No problem, sir. Just to let you know I have a firearm in the car and I do have my CPL license", I informed the officer.

"In my system it shows that your tags are outdated", he said to me.

"That's impossible, I paid for them last year for my birthday, plus you see that the tags are the right color", I said aggressively.

The officer went to his car for about 20 minutes. In my rearview mirror, I saw another cop car pulling up. "Are you serious?", I said aloud.

The officer came back to my vehicle while the other officer was on the other side holding a flash light to my face. "Can you please step out of the car?

"What did I do wrong, sir?", I asked.

"Your registration is outdated, and your tags are old, so we have to confiscate the car", he said.

"What? That's impossible. You have my information in your hand that shows my paperwork is up to date", I told the officer.

"Well, my system shows something different", he responded.

I thought to myself that this was a prime example of racial profiling and unjust acts by the police. I asked the officer if it was okay to grab my firearm and he said, "if the license checks out, then you will be fine". After searching my car for drugs or alcohol, he asked, "Is there anything you need to grab before the tow truck gets here?"

Now I was pissed off because I just went shopping for my Miami trip the next day and I was standing outside the car with bags of stuff just getting rained on. I thought to myself, *this could not get any worse.*

Then, the officer came up to me and said, "Because you did not immediately state that you had a firearm, by law I have to confiscate that to". I was livid and wanted to curse the officer out, but I knew that as a black man in America and being aggressive with the police always leads to a tragic ending.

I called my friend to come pick me up, so I could explain to her what just happened to me. With nowhere to go and lay my head, I felt hopeless. So, we got a room and she took me to the airport in the morning. In Miami, I made sure I did not think of all of my struggles when I linked up with my line brothers. Lots of drinking, partying and great vibes. An overdue vacation that was needed. The day I got back to Detroit it hit me that I did not have a car in my possession. I took off work to go handle the car and firearm situation. After the court visits and lawyer fees, I ended up paying over $3,000.00 for a crime I did not commit.

After 6 months of being homeless, on June 14th, 2017, I was finally able to sign a lease to a two-bedroom house on 8 Mile and Southfield Road, a quiet neighborhood, and after introducing myself to a few neighbors I felt confident about moving in. I walked in the house after I got the keys from the leasing office and I rejoiced. "God, I knew you would come through on your word. You said to be ye steadfast and to have faith in your promises. Thank you for following through and delivering like you always do", I was shouting around the house. It felt so good to finally have a place to call my own.

In the last six months of being homeless, my relationship with my brother had diminished, my car and firearm got taken, I was charged for crimes I did not commit, I missed out on opportunities because I was not prepared, and it seemed that my life was stagnant for a very long time. Even through the storm, I stayed positive because I knew that one day God would deliver on his word.

After a week of living in the new place, I decided to go to Atlanta for my line brothers Tyler and Kenneth's birthday. I flew down on June 22nd, 2017 to celebrate with them because we never missed each other's birthday. We had so much fun partying and fellowshipping with great people. I came to celebrate them, but they were so happy that I'd found a place to stay so they were celebrating me as well. I remember boarding the plane and thanking God that I had a home to go to when I got back.

I arrived home on Sunday June 25th, 2017, around 2 p.m. I pulled up in my driveway and noticed that my side gate was open. I did not think much of it at the time. I walked in the house and set my bags down to use the bathroom. As I was walking through the hallway, I noticed that my closet door was open, so I glanced in it and nothing was in there. I rushed to my room and my face dropped. Someone had broken into my house and stolen all of my things. Six months of being homeless and within 11 days someone wiped me of everything that I had. My clothes, MacBook, jewelry, 55-inch television, shoes and my change stash of $67.54.

The first thing I began to do was pray. "Dear God, thank you for being God. Thank you for not allowing anyone to be home while this took place because you know that I carry, and someone probably would have died so thank you. I do not understand why this has happened to me, but you said in your word to lean not on your own understanding. I pray that whoever has my belongings appreciates this blessing of nice things. In Jesus name, I say amen". I did not call my brother or mother crying, nor was I upset. The Bible says in Philippians 2:14, "Do everything without grumbling and complaining".

I called my brother and told him about the devastating news and he could not believe it. I asked him if I could come back for a few days to figure some things out and he said yes. Two more months passed of the same cycle. In and out of my brother's house, sleeping in my car, looking up houses every day on my phone, setting up appointments and getting disappointed with my findings. I had to remain positive because I was preaching it on Instagram every day. Although I was going through hell, I was still speaking at events, inspiring people on my social platforms, walking around with a smile and making impact within my community.

On August 19th, 2017, I got an opportunity to purchase a home. *At the age of 26 I could be a homeowner?* That's what I was thinking to myself. I found a house in Oak Park, Michigan, which was a better community than the last place that I lived in for 11 days. The paperwork got approved and I could not do anything but thank God for coming through again.

Then it hit me, I was thinking lease, but God was thinking buy. I was thinking rent but God was thinking own. Sometimes in life, the reasons why we get rejected and our plans do not go the way we envision them is because we are thinking too small. I did not share my experience with too many people because I did not want anyone to have empathy for me. I learned in 2017 that your life can change in one year. Also, you do not have to look like what you are going through. With all of the adversity that I was dealing with, it gave me a different level of passion for what I love to do. It was blessing to help so many people with my words that it got around and I was getting booked left and right.

So, although I was going through one of the worst times in my life, God was still blessing me with my career abundantly. I was able to book the most speaking engagements I have ever had within the same year. 2017 also taught me that when you ask God for a breakthrough, you have to be prepared to go through something. Going through storms is not a bad thing, embrace the storm. The problem is not going through the storm; the problem is when you park. When you park in your storm, you begin to look around at how hard the wind is blowing and how loud the thunder is, which will frighten you. It is physically and spiritually impossible to have a breakthrough without going through it first. So, when someone tells me they are going through it, I respond with, "You are in a great position because what is on the other side of the breakthrough is far greater than what you are going through". I knew that from this moment forward, after I took my next step in life, there would be no going back.

CHAPTER 11: YOUR LIFE'S ELEVATOR

I believe that life is about making choices, persevering through life's adversity and forward progression. Your life's elevation is like an elevator, but before you can increase the level of your perspective, you can start by following an equation that I have created: Elevation = Isolation + Restoration + Transformation.

Some people may look at isolation as being lonely, alienated and in a depressed state of mind. Isolation is where you find yourself! Not only will you find yourself, but you can fall in love with yourself. You can understand and calculate your self-worth through isolation. That way you will never sell yourself short in life. It's hard to have a clear vision of your life's purpose if you're always around others because their values, beliefs, insecurities and actions influence yours. Once you truly understand who you are, no one can skew your vision! Being alone you will find out what you're good at, what you're marginalized at and what you suck at. Living up to the expectations of other people will never bring you self-identity, which can lead to confusion, frustration and depression.

I remember graduating from college as a distinguished college student. I was very popular, a member of the prestigious Alpha Phi Alpha Fraternity Incorporated, Founder of my own organization F.A.M.I.L.Y. (Forget About Me, I Love You), student activist and mentor. Nine days after I walked across the stage I relocated to Merrillville, Indiana, where I had no family, friends or clue as to where I was moving to for my new start at a steel company. I was not sure what to expect from my new journey and I had no clue that I was officially starting my isolation process. It was a struggle, my job that I signed a contract for was nothing I'd expected it to be. The plant life did not mesh well with my engineering skills. The city was very industrialized so there was not enough civilization to my liking. Due to the lack of friends and family there I never went out to socialize, so I began to feel alienated from the world.

After two months of repeating the same cycle of going to work at a place I hated and returning home, I decided to spend more quality time with myself. I started to evaluate my life by asking myself a few questions: *Who is Keyon Clinton? What is my purpose in life? What do I value? What is my brand? Am I currently happy with my life right now?* After my self-assessment, I concluded that I had no idea who I was at 25 years old. I had spent so much time trying to live up to others' expectations that I did not set any for myself. I was battling with facing my true reality versus the facade that I had been living in for the last 25 years of my life.

Two more months went by and, after battling with myself, I finally gave in and accepted the fact that it was time for me to dig deep and find myself so that I could be happy internally. The first step was now accomplished, and I began moving forward in my process. I had to accept that I had some weaknesses that needed immediate attention and I had some strengths that I needed to continue to exude. Through this isolation period I was able to fall in love with myself, figure out what I wanted to do in life, envision the type of people I wanted to be around and work with, what I wanted my brand to be and, most importantly be authentically me.

What I realized was that there are two sides to every experience that you endure. At first being alone was scary for me because of what I was familiar to. My mind was not conditioned to think for myself and value myself without the input of others. I struggled because I did not like what I saw when I looked in the mirror and faced my truth. Imagine a headshot of you with nothing but all your flaws, insecurities and mistakes on it. That's exactly how I looked at 25 years old. Once I was able to shift my perspective, I stopped looking at my flaws as negative things and started seeing them as an opportunity to better myself. Now that I had been introduced to the first part of the equation unexpectedly, I was very intentional with the next step of restoration.

Restoration comes after you find yourself! Now you can set clear goals that align with your purpose. You can intervene and assess your life's path and see where you made some mistakes and how you will grow from them. Then, you can build upon your life's foundation and create a custom-tailored path toward your purpose in life. Just knowing who you are and where you want to be (which comes from isolation) isn't always enough. Restoration helps you create the goals, timeline, checkpoints, etc. so that you can be efficient and effective in who you are. After you figure out who you are, your value to the world and what your plans in life are, you have to begin restoring your life so that the bigger picture becomes clearer. I truly believe that God has given all of us the necessary tools and equipment to be successful in life. We just need to know how to use them effectively. God has given us love, confidence, willpower, a voice and his word to protect us on this journey. Knowing what you want to do in life is good but knowing how you are going to do it is even better.

Five months into my new journey I was aware of who I was and what I wanted to do. I decided to go to Walmart and buy three whiteboards and I labeled them Goals, Vision, and Hobbies/Interests. When I left Michigan State University, I was one of the most popular guys there because of my involvement on campus and within nine days I became invisible to the real world. None of my accolades and accomplishments mattered to corporate America and that showed me that I was living up to everybody else's expectations and not my own. I had no idea what goals I wanted to accomplish, no vision of how I wanted to be known and no original hobbies and interests of my own.

Just when I gained the courage to be who I was, I was hit with another road block of reality. I could not believe that after 25 years I could not figure out one goal in life. I felt the depression coming back, but this time I told myself, *I am bigger than depression and I have to dig deeper to figure my life out.* I asked myself, based off my values, what my strengths were and what I believed in, and what I could do that would accommodate these things. My non-profit organization F.A.M.I.L.Y. involved working with people, impacting youth and rebuilding the community which were all things I loved to do so I figured I would go full throttle with this endeavor. I prayed to God that night and asked him, if this was his calling for my life allow me to succeed in it.

I woke up the next day inspired to embark upon my new journey. I started planning the vision for the non-profit; I thought of the people I wanted to serve on the executive board, events that I planned out for the entire year and potential business partnerships that would be beneficial to my success. The more I fell in love with the process the clearer my vision became. I started to write out my goals on the whiteboard and create the vision as to how I was going to do it.

So, after all this planning and strategizing reality sunk in again. I was in a place that was uncomfortable. I could not get started in Indiana with no family, friends, connections and little civilization. Once again, another road block of reality hit me. As the days went by, I found myself getting frustrated and feeling stuck in a bad place with a great idea.

I started to fill out job applications to move back home to Detroit so that I could be around my family, friends and familiarity. I filled out 10 applications a week because I was determined to find a job back home. As an electrical engineer, with a good GPA and 4 internships and 1 co-op of experience there was no way I would not get a phone call for an interview. No matter how great of a resume I thought I had it was clear that corporations thought differently because I did not receive one phone call. I had to find an outlet so that I could cope with the rejection that I had been receiving.

One day, I got out of the shower and I finally looked in the mirror and had a disgusted look on my face. I was so displeased with what I saw, and I could not believe that I had let myself go. I began to lose confidence in myself. So, I decided to start my fitness and health journey because I believe that if you look good, you will feel good. If you feel good, you will produce better results in life. I asked myself, "Keyon, what do you want to achieve when it's all said and done?". Instantly I told myself I wanted to "trim the fat". I wanted to trim the fat so that I could have a nice physique when I wore custom-tailored suits and I wanted to trim the fat so that I could be healthy enough to see 90 years old without a cane or any other health-related issues.

So, it began; I started running, I was in the gym daily throughout the week and I even changed some eating habits because summer was here, and I wanted to trim the fat so that I could stop being the guy at the pool parties with my shirt on inside of the pool. I was working hard in the gym whenever I would go, I was consistently going 3 to 4 days a week, but on the weekends the turn up was real! I was driving back home, drinking, partying, up all night, hanging around the wrong crowd of people, but on Monday I was right back to the regimen of hard work and consistency.

Now, if you paid attention to my regimen I would work hard in the gym and stay consistent throughout the week, but I lacked the discipline to reach my desired fitness goals. I became frustrated to the point where I fell into another deep depression. I lost my confidence; my spirits were always down, and I alienated myself from my loved ones. Then, one day, as I was having an intervention with myself after realizing that my life was not going the way I had always intended it to go, I asked myself a question. I said, "Keyon, what do you need to do to get back to living a purposeful life?" I instantly told myself that I needed to "trim the fat" in my life! So, I hit the gym again and this time I was going extra hard and staying consistent. After a month, I saw that I had lost a few pounds, so I was feeling good about myself because I was focused during the weekends. I knew that if I built a better physique I would restore my confidence, which will directly and indirectly affect other areas of my life.

This continued journey in fitness allowed me to cope with my circumstance of being in a place I was uncomfortable in at first. I prayed to God and told him that I accepted the position I was in and I asked that he show me the reason as to why I was here.

One morning, I woke up feeling renewed. My perspective on things were different because I had stopped complaining and started being appreciative of the things I did have; a job, car, place to stay, money and health. Two weeks later, I heard from DTE ENERGY about an interview. Feelings of joy and excitement coursed through my body. I prepared and crushed the phone interview and a one week later was offered a position to come back home and work with DTE ENERGY. In that moment, I realized that God took me through that 9-month process of being uncomfortable so that I could grow spiritually, mentally and physically.

HEALING THE LIVING DEAD

I remember sitting in the living room in my apartment in Merrillville, Indiana, thinking of my entire process; then revelation came to me. In 9 months, a mother gives birth to a child. As the mother goes through the different trimesters, the child is growing. Sometimes in life you will be in uncomfortable positions and feeling limited in your ability to show your true self to the world because you have to endure the process first. Growth takes time. I was very uncomfortable through that 9-month period, I felt constrained and stuck at times, and without family and friends I felt like I was all alone in this dark space and when I finally accepted my position in life and reached a peak of growth throughout this process, I was provided with an opportunity to have a fresh start. Then it hit me, God was birthing me for a new platform that I was not ready for 9 months ago. Being isolated, restoring my confidence and growing spiritually, mentally and physically had prepared me for the last variable of the equation of elevation.

Transformation is the byproduct of isolation and restoration! Once you know who you are, what your purpose is and how you're going to do it, now all you have to do is implement your vision into a reality and, through hard work, consistency and discipline, you will magnify your transformation. When your mind is conditioned to think at a higher level and your actions speak louder than your words, your transformation will be in full effect. People around you will be affected by change, the community around you will be affected by change and the world around you will be affected by change!

After working my last two weeks with ArcelorMittal and packing my things to move back home I reminisced one more time about the experience that I had endured over this time. "Thank you for my rebirth, God" were the last words I said in that apartment.

On my way back home, all I could think about was how refreshing moving back home would be. I was moving back in with my mother, so I was not too excited about that because over the last 10 years I had my own freedom, but I figured it would work out since we are both happy that I was there. The first weekend back home I had dinner with my family and friends to celebrate. The amount of love and good fellowship warmed my heart. I just knew that life was about to move toward an upward incline. I remember praying and asking God to transform my mind so that I could take my life to the next level. After I prayed I just sat there and waited on a response from God. My grandmother always used to say, "Be careful what you ask for because you just might get it". I feel asleep and, in my dream, God told me to stop running my non-profit organization and start speaking his name across the world. I woke up at 4:22 a.m. in a cold sweat. "God, I asked you to take me to the next level, not take away my purpose", is what I said to him. The next morning, I was frustrated. I could not believe that everything that I had built over the last 2 years God wanted me to just stop. I was literally torn between my flesh and my spirit. As much as I trusted God, I told him no. I wanted to grow my non-profit around Detroit and bless thousands of youth all over because I just knew I had a good thing going for myself. Also, speaking publicly was not my forte. I was so afraid to get up in front of a crowd and say a few words so why would God want to embarrass me like that? I thought of every way not to speak and instead work on my non-profit, but I could not get approved for any funding; I could not book any spaces, some of the people I started with backed out on me and before I knew it F.A.M.I.L.Y. was not in a good position. I got on my knees and said, "God, I have been disobedient, and I ask for your forgiveness. I tried to do things my way, but I know that it's your will not my will be done. I fully surrender to you and I will walk by faith and not by sight". That same night God showed me visions of me speaking in front of millions of people.

I woke up the following morning startled from the vision I had the night before, I knew I had to get to work. Paradigms were shifted in my mind, which caused me to think differently. I knew my self-worth, I also knew where I wanted to go and the people I want to impact; now it was time to implement and execute so that I could transform into the man God called me to be. I used my leverage on Instagram to begin my speaking career.

At first, I was just sharing my thoughts on current topics that I had interest in. As the buzz began to build up I gained more confidence in my ability and purpose. I knew I had to create a message, brand, logo and movement in order to sustain in this field. I did my research on speaking, studied the greats who came before me and started building my connections with people who would assist me on this journey. Before I knew it, I was getting booked to speak at different places. Once my mindset changed, my character changed and that is when I started seeing major results in my life. Once you have defined and implemented the three components of isolation, restoration and transformation, I can guarantee you that your life will continue to elevate to new platforms and plateaus forever!

Elevation is like an elevator! Once you make your mind up that you're ready to elevate your life, you have to start with the basics! Once you isolate yourself you are now officially on ground level. Before you can move to a higher place in life you must accept who and where you are right now in life. Once you have clearly defined yourself (you know who you are and who you truly want to be in life) you then can begin restoring your life. Yes, you have encountered detours in life (some of which you've taken on your own will) but you're ready to learn and grow from your previous mistakes and habits. While restoring yourself, you can set attainable goals for your life! You can begin building the infrastructure to the blue print you have created in your isolation phase. Through hard work, consistency and discipline your mindset will begin to transform causing everything else around you to transform as well. Once you confess, "I know where I am in life, I know where I want to be, I have a plan on how I will get there, and my mindset is conditioned to let nothing, or no one stop me from getting there", that is when you can feel your life beginning to elevate!

The ground floor is always the most amazing floor because you will vividly see how your transformed mind can take you to new heights, new platforms and plateaus and it feels amazing! This is usually where you communicate your vision to all of your family, friends and close confidants. They are excited to experience the "new" and transformed you. They tell you that they are here for you, you can trust and depend on them to help you rise to the next level of life. (Ding Second Floor)

If you have not figured it out, my friends, elevation is like an elevator because the higher you go up in life the more doors and opportunities will open for you. As these doors and opportunities open, more people will come into your life unexpectedly to help you go to the next level. Now, the beauty of the elevator is that when these doors open, and you have reached a new level of perspective, not only will people come into your life, but some people will walk out of your life as well. In the beginning these are your family members, friends and confidants who promised to be by your side for the long run, but they realized that you have changed! You are not the same person you used to be anymore. You do not condone things that do not add value or substance to your life and it is too much for them to accept so they walk out. Although it may hurt you to see them go you must understand that, in life, in order to elevate you must sometimes evacuate! God will remove people who do not belong in your life no matter what significance they hold in your life. Now you are sad and hurt because you believed that your loved ones would have been there with you until the end, but you do not even realize what God is doing for your life!

First, thank him for your ability to have reached new heights. Secondly, there were some unexpected people who have entered your life and that are about to bless you! You do not know who they are or where they came from, but in due time you will realize that they are the pieces to the puzzle that you've been missing. (Ding Third Floor)

More doors! More opportunities! More people in! More people out! The higher you go in life the higher your level of perspective becomes. You have enough sense now to let people walk out of your life who are not willing to invest in your purpose, but you have more confidence that the people who are on this elevator with you will continue to help you elevate. (Ding Fourth Floor)

Now, as crazy as this may sound, some people do not like the feeling of elevation. As their life is rising with yours it affects them and can cause a bubbly feeling in their stomach so they have to get off because they feel sick or insecure that you are increasing and they are not. You cannot wait on them because these people were solely meant to help you on that specific level of life that you were on. Yes, that is great, but they were not meant to go to the next level with you. Now, as your life is rising, and you are feeling good, just remember that things go wrong as they sometimes will. The elevator gets stuck, now what do you do? Do you become resistant or do you become resourceful? Are you going to complain about how life sucks because you have hit a road block in your growth and focus on the negatives of your life or are you going to remain positive, utilize the people who are in your life and figure out a plan to get this elevator back on track?

Sometimes God places you in a position of life where you cannot do anything but call for help. Once you get back on track with your elevation process you have learned to value the people who stuck around when you had a down moment in life. As you continue to experience your life's elevator you fall in love with the process because you understand that results may vary. When you get to the top floor, which is your floor of purpose, and those doors open up, you look up in the right corner of the elevator and see a capacity sign. In that moment, it all makes sense to you that everybody could not have gone with you. So, you just thank God for your elevation, and because you are so generous of your process you send the elevator down for the next person to start their elevation process.

HEALING THE LIVING DEAD

PHASE 3: ELEVATION

<u>WEALTHY HABITS</u>

Success does not happen overnight. It is a process that is achieved through your daily habits. All successful people have routines that they follow every day to sustain their success. I am going to provide you with 11 habits that will shift paradigms within you, which will allow you to elevate your level of perspective. Implementing these habits will shift you from a "Morgue" mentality to a "Forbes" mentality. When people hear Forbes they instantly think of money. From my experience of talking and connecting with people who made the Forbes list and being mentored by someone who sits on the coaching counsel for Forbes, it is more about having a wealthy mindset. The habits that I am providing will help you spiritually, mentally and physically so that you can become the best version of yourself. The

195

"Morgue" mentally is a poverty mindset of not believing you can be phenomenal and after implementing these habits, I can guarantee that you will have gained the confidence to conquer any obstacle that you are faced with in life.

1) *Always Put God First In Everything You Do!* I am a firm believer that if God is the primary source of any endeavor in your life, it will work out in your favor. Having a spiritual connection with a higher source allows your mind, body and soul to flourish in ways that the human mind cannot fathom. Putting God first also humbles you. Showing humility builds character and I believe that your character will take you further in life than any gift or talent you possess. Proverbs 3:9 says, "Honor the LORD with your wealth, with the first fruits

of all your crops". So, it's not just beneficial to praise God when you are going through something but to give God the best part of everything that you produce. Exalting God first in everything you do helps builds your faith. Faith gives you the understanding that you may not know how you are going to get through your circumstances, but you know that, with God by your side, you have nothing to worry about. Science tells us that when we try to elevate in the air, gravity holds us down. From a spiritually perspective, when we try to elevate in God, the enemy tries to hold us down. Just as there are certain parameters we need to elevate in air, we must have parameters to elevate in God. Faith, trust, love, a relationship and knowledge of the Bible are the parameters that will allow us to grow in God consistently. Although human vision can be 20/20, as we age our eyesight begins to get blurry. The vision you get from God never diminishes. This is why putting God first in everything you do will increase your level of perspective.

2) ***Create Your Own Personal Mission Statement!*** Everybody should have a "code" that they live by. The United States of America has one with the Pledge of Allegiance and businesses have one, so why don't you? This is your personal mission statement. A personal mission statement provides clarity and gives you a sense of purpose. It defines who you are and how you will live. There arc 5 questions that I challenge you to answer before creating your own personal mission statement:

a) What is important? What/Whom do you value? How is your life connected to those things? Are you prioritizing your priorities?

b) Where do you want to go in life? First identify where you are currently in life and accept it! Create your vision of the bigger picture in life. Once that is finished, then start formulating the path that it will take to get there step by step (include spiritually, mentally, physically, emotionally, financially and any other aspect of your life).

c) What does "the best version of you" look like?". Describe your "moon shot" version of yourself. Don't base this off of your current situation, think big! You have the ability to create your own future because you control your own destiny. Do not short-change yourself.

d) What do you want your brand to be? Your brand is your image, your message, your platform and how people will describe you. Think of what information will pop up when your name is googled. Having a great brand will produce success in many aspects of your life.

e) What kind of legacy do you want to leave behind? No one will live forever so what will you leave behind when you are gone? Ask yourself when you die do you want an obituary or a documentary? The lives you touch and the impact you have while you are on earth can inspire generations after you. That is an exciting thought, right? Start now because what you do today will affect your tomorrow. Once you answer these 5 questions you will be able to develop a concise and powerful mission statement that will provide you with clarity on living a purposeful life.

3) ***Positivity Triumphs ALL!*** *A*lways keep a positive mindset no matter what you are going through in life. I am not saying it makes the problem go away but I can guarantee that you will have a more rational thinking and healthier approach when you are hit with life's blows. Being positive in life is one of the things you can control, and by exuding this at all times no one will ever have control over your energy. Being positive allows you to control your emotions. Controlling your emotions will alleviate unnecessary stress, arguments, disappointments and heartbreaks. Also, being positive gives you a high level of confidence to be the great person that you truly are. An optimistic mind keeps you thinking forward, and

a pessimistic mind focuses on the problem instead of the solution.

4) ***YOU Can Be Great In Your Situation!*** No matter what your current circumstances are you can be great in that moment. You do not have to wait until you reach a certain platform, nor do you need the validity and affirmation of others to believe that you can be great. People sometimes fail to realize that there is growth in their struggle. The moment you decide that you are ready to ascend to a higher level that is when your life's perspective will begin to increase. Another thing to understand is that it is not about where you are currently in life but where God is leading you to. On your journey to success you will encounter detours, hardships and rejection. You must always believe and never give up.

There is revelation in your struggle. Hard times show you your character. Embrace where you are in life and use your current situation as inspiration to keep striving for greatness.

5) ***Concepts NEVER Change!*** The term "There's nothing new under the sun" is true. We all have struggles and hardships, but the challenge is how are you turning your negatives into positives? Exert the same energy and effort into a positive atmosphere and watch as you reap the benefits of success. For example, I joined a gang in the streets because I wanted to be a part of a group of people with likeminded tendencies; I wanted a brotherhood and I wanted to be accepted by some men who would not judge me for my flaws. When I went to college, I joined a fraternity because I wanted to be a part

of a group of people with likeminded tendencies, I wanted a brotherhood and I wanted to be accepted by some men who would not judge me for my flaws. Understanding this habit will not only give you knowledge, but it helps you apply the knowledge that you have. Trust the process because the results will vary. Concepts serve as the principles you value, which will build discipline to keep you from skewing your vision in life.

6) *Winners Are Proactive, Losers Are Reactive!* You cannot control the hand you were dealt, but you can control two things: 1) how you play your cards and 2) what your "poker" face will show. Successful people do not sit around and wait for life to happen to them, they create a path on their own to live! Being proactive

challenges your mind to stay two steps ahead. I always tell myself that it is better to be prepared and not need anything than to need something and not be prepared. The key is to be proactive in everything you do. For example, Networking; once you meet someone, a proactive mindset will follow up within 48 hours and a reactive mindset will wait for the other contact to reach out to them. A proactive mind is a confident mind. Bad experiences will not produce bad thoughts in your head if you are a proactive person because you are focused on how you can improve from that experience.

7) ***Build "Potluck" Relationships!*** All relationships should be fruitful. The best way to ensure that everybody is gaining and benefiting from the relationship is to "bring something to the table". If you have a one-way

relationship where you are the one who is always giving, always going the extra mile, then eventually the relationship will die out. All parties will feast if everybody brought something to the table. When building relationships, not only should you bring something to the table, but you should serve what you brought to the other parties first before receiving things from the other parties. That shows the humility in you as a person. By having relationships with reciprocity, mutuality and love, there is a great chance that your relationship with that person will continue to thrive.

8) ***Treat Success Like a Puzzle!*** When you create your vision and finally see the bigger picture in life, it is only the beginning. You then have to remove the cover of your vision and begin putting the pieces of the puzzle

together. Success is not a straight path; you will encounter detours, you will become frustrated and you will get rejected on your path to success, but you must never give up. If you truly want to be successful, never seek success. Seek to become a person of value because when you become a valuable person in life, people will seek your presence. When you put all of the pieces of your puzzle together to achieve success, realize that you are the final piece that makes your vision come to life.

9) ***Consistency Always Wins!*** Life is a marathon not a sprint. We live in a world where temporary satisfaction is becoming the norm in society. Success in any facet of life requires you to be consistent. Remain consistent in your endeavors; stay congruent on your journey to achieving your life goals. Even when you do not feel like it, when

you're exhausted or when you are ready to give up, keep going, don't stop! Some people have been consistent on their path to success, but they are becoming weary because it seems as if their hard work is in vain. You are not doing anything wrong, the timing and position just have not presented themselves for your vision to become your reality. The moment is already ordained by God, you just have to be prepared for it. Matthew 24:13 says, "But he that shall endure unto the end, the same shall be saved".

10)   ***Not Every Great Opportunity Is Your Opportunity!***

When you are walking in your purpose, you understand that you must have tunnel vision. Realize that everything you do must align with your mission and core values; it has to make sense to you. With this mindset, you understand that not every great opportunity is your opportunity. It is easy to get caught up in trying to execute on all of your great ideas, but when you prioritize your priorities, you will learn the value of saying no! Those who try to be good at everything will never be great at anything. You will find yourself stretched too thin to fully impact the world in the capacity you were built for if you say yes to every opportunity presented your way. Purpose has an alignment that correlates with the assignment that you were given by God. Once you are fully walking in your purpose, anything that does not align with your assignment will be a distraction.

11)   ***Treat Future Generations Like Seeds!*** Ask yourself, "How do seeds grow?", First you have plant them in the right soil. It is imperative to place our youth in the right atmosphere that will fertilize their thinking which will

build the roots of courage and confidence. Then seeds need water and sunlight. Pour into and shed light on their ideas so that they are confident enough to share their visions with the entire world. When the windstorms of hardships, trials and tribulations come their way, they will not stumble, nor will they fall because they will be standing on the barks of commitment. In due time, you will reap the ripe fruit borne of their trees of success due to the content of their character. The youth is the future, so it is imperative that you invest in as many lives as you can. The return on your investment is changing the trajectory of those people's lives. This place a high level of obligation on you to be an example for others, which means you will live with integrity and wisdom.

BECOMING 1% BETTER

As an advocate for execution who delivers life-changing messages, I believe that every day when we wake up we should ask ourselves a simple question. "How can I become at least 1% better today?". Through faith, go deeper in your prayers and study more of your word. Through fitness, go harder in the gym and stay consistent with healthy eating. Through self-discovery, finding out exactly who you are and who you want to be and then starting to walk in your true purpose. Whatever it is, whatever it takes, just sacrifice and execute. If you start today, I can guarantee you that in 1 year from now you will have increased the efficiency in your daily operation by 365%. That means that you will think on a different level, you will move on a different level and most importantly you will win on a different level.

When you focus on the little things in life, you will begin to pay attention to detail. Paying attention to detail increases your efficiency in the way you execute. Execution builds the drive in a person. The more driven you are the more determined in life you will be.

I believe that a driven person is more effective than a motivated person. Motivation is like taking a controlled substance. Yes, you will feel high and motivated for a moment, but after a while your buzz will begin to dwindle down. The only way to get back on a high is to get some more motivation. There are people who have to listen to motivational speeches and music to get it going. There is nothing wrong with getting a dose of encouraging words but when things go wrong and your plans do not work out, motivation tends to leave. A person who is driven understands that, no matter what happens, they must execute. Ask yourself what are you driven by? These answers are usually things that hold true value in your life like your relationship with God, family, your upbringing, etc.

Goal setting is another way to accomplish your goals in life. Goals serve as the GPS to your end destination, which is purpose. Once you find your purpose you then have to start walking in it every day. Creating goals is not enough. To become 1% better in goal setting you must create daily goals. When the New Year comes around everybody seems to have a New Year's resolution with their goals for the year. What I have noticed is that goals without deadlines do not put the pressure on you that you need to reach them efficiently. Daily goals will keep you aligned with your yearly goals so that you do not skew your vision along the way.

Lastly, your daily routine determines the longevity in your success. Here is my daily routine of how I become 1% better every day. I wake up to my alarm at 6am. I purposely placed my phone on the opposite side of the room so that I have to get out of the bed to turn off my alarm. Next to my phone I have a bottle of water to drink so that my body gets hydrated. This prevents me from hitting snooze and lying back in the bed. I spend my quality time praying to God so that my spirit is right. I then go to the bathroom, brush my teeth and wash my face. I look in the mirror and begin speaking my affirmations to myself. "Keyon, you are a king, you deserve greatness. You will bless someone today. Today will be a great day. Your life matters. Now go be 1% better today". I speak these affirmations because we live in a world where people will tell you the opposite of good things every day. They will project their fears, doubts and insecurities onto you if you allow them to. I value time, so I make sure that my clothes are ironed the night before so that I do not spend unnecessary time in the morning ironing. Once I am dressed, I review my daily goals to go over my game plan for the day.

I step out of the house and my mind is already set on success because I have already affirmed it within myself. So, everything I do is intentional, and I am very productive.

It is the routine that builds efficiency and effectiveness within your daily operation. I challenge you to create a daily routine and try it for 30 days and watch how much more productive you will become. Becoming 1% better in everything that you do will change your life because you will value the little things, pay close attention to detail and always continue moving forward in life.

Now that I have shared my life's testimony and habits to wealthy living with you, I pray that you find the strength in your story to become 1% better every day. It is now up to you to apply everything you learned and live the great life God has called you to live.

About the Author

From a drug dealer to a soul healer, Keyon Clinton has found a way to turn his negatives into positives. Graduating from Michigan State University with his degree in Electrical Engineering, working for a multibillion-dollar company, he is a self-published author, Execution Coach, Professional Speaker, Founder of a non-profit organization Forget About Me, I Love You! (F.A.M.I.L.Y.) and Certified Bodybuilder. Keyon Clinton is born and raised in Detroit Michigan and he believes that every person's life can be elevated and today he is here to increase your level of perspective.

He has been featured and hosted segments with Channel 4 WDIV Detroit News, Fox 2 Detroit News, WKAR Radio Station, The State News, Small Talk with Mark Lee, WXYT

1270 Radio Station, COBO Hall, Ford Field and the Magic Johnson Foundation.

Keyon Clinton is a 2018 receipt of *The Top 25 Millennials in Detroit.* He speaks extensively on the subjects of seeking God first, execution, purpose, consistency, leadership and healthy relationships. He empowers people at schools, colleges, churches, corporations, conferences and community centers by inspiring others to become 1% better every day.

Keyon Clinton grew up in Detroit, Michigan and is a proud product of 48205.

Connect with Keyon Clinton

To request Keyon Clinton for speaking engagements,

media interviews, or for bulk book purchases, please

email: KeyonClintonSpeaks@gmail.com

Website:

www.KeyonClintonSpeaks.com

Social Media

facebook.com/KeyonClinton

instagram.com/KeyonClintonSpeaks

twitter.com/KeyonClintonSpeaks

#HealingTheLivingDead

HEALING THE LIVING DEAD

26332359R00138

Made in the USA
Columbia, SC
08 September 2018